THE BREAK UP MANUAL FOR MEN

RECOVER FROM A SERIOUS BREAK UP, BECOME STRONGER AND GET YOUR EX BACK (IF YOU WANT)

ANDREW FEREBEE

Founder of KnowledgeForMen.com

The Break Up Manual For Men
Recover From a Serious Breakup, Become Stronger and Get Your Ex Back (If You Want)

By Andrew Ferebee

ISBN-13: 9798358006560

Legal Disclaimer:

This book is dedicated to the man suffering through one of the most confusing and painful times of his life—the loss of a lover. May this book bring you strength, peace, and clarity on your journey forward.

CONTENTS

INTRODUCTION

WHY I WROTE THIS

I know what it's like to mourn the loss of someone you love, someone who is still alive, well, and likely living only a few miles away.

I know what it's like to have your entire world flipped upside down without warning. You might have felt like you're on the path to "till death do us part," only to blindsided and the woman you love transform before your eyes. She morphs from being your lover, your partner, and your best friend into a cold and distant stranger.

Then it comes:

"I'm just not in love with you anymore."

Maybe you were drifting apart as the lackluster date nights and sexless nights became commonplace, or you were in a state of romantic harmony only to be betrayed by infidelity or her sudden need for space. Maybe you saw the breakup looming on the horizon long before it happened, but it was too late for any meaningful change.

I know how you feel right now. I've been there. More importantly, I know how to successfully navigate the path ahead of you.

You see, over the years, I've experienced the highest highs and lowest lows in my relationships. Sure, I've been broken up with, cheated on, and left crying myself to sleep after the woman I thought I was going to marry left me for another man just weeks after the breakup.

I've made every mistake a man can make during the relationship, in the weeks leading up to the breakup, during the breakup, and after it. I've begged on my knees, pleaded, and given away my power. I've tried numbing my pain with alcohol, porn, drugs, and a flood of empty sex.

But I've also learned from my mistakes. I've screwed up really bad so that you don't have to.

After fifteen years of trial and error, falling in and out of love, experiencing failure, triumph, pain, and euphoria, I've discovered that there is a roadmap to recovery. Even better, it's an almost step-by-step process that men can use to reclaim their power, their confidence, and their sense of worth after a breakup. Best of all, if both of you believe it's the right decision, there's even a system to rekindle the attraction with "the one that got away."

I was able to transmute the pain of my worst breakup into the fuel I needed to reinvent myself as a man and rebuild my life from the ground up. By following the strategies and action steps I'm going to share in this book, you can too.

And it all started exactly where you're sitting right now—in the wake of a devastating breakup. Alone. Depressed. Lost. In pain.

I went through life on autopilot, tossing and turning at night, unable to sleep without an IV drip of liquor. By day, I walked the streets like a zombie with its heart ripped out, stumbling around my daily life with a fake smile. The things that once brought me joy and excitement had lost all luster and meaning. Through it all, I was left wondering if I would ever feel as happy again as I had with her.

Today, I'm the founder of Knowledge for Men, the host of the top-ranked podcast by the same name, the author of the bestselling book The Dating Playbook for Men, and the creator of a leading men's coaching program that has changed thousands of men's lives around the world.

I've created the preeminent personal transformation system helping men reclaim their power and become stronger more Grounded Men. I've been privileged to live a life that many people (including my former self) would describe as "unreal." I went from stocking shelves at the local grocery store to building a leading men's coaching organization that's impacted millions of men around the world.

In my personal life, I went from struggling to make eye contact with strangers to dating high-quality women that most would assume were out of my league.

I've gone from feeling trapped in the "groundhog day" of an un-lived life to traveling the world, getting in the best shape of my life, building an elite social network, and waking up each morning feeling a level of aliveness that I didn't know was possible without substances. It's taken me from feeling weak, purposeless, and emasculated as a man to reclaiming my power, discovering my truth, and reigniting the fire in my belly to create the career, social life, and relationships I thought was reserved for other men.

Ultimately, you will soon realize that this "crisis" is actually an opportunity for your greatest transformation as a man and is a necessary experience in order to uncover the life changing lessons that will shape the rest of your life.

You may not believe me right now, but this is happening for you, not against you. Trust the process.

THE GOAL OF THIS BOOK

I never planned to share *anything* you're about to read.

This project started as a way for *me* to distill the lessons and mistakes I was learning throughout my breakups so that I could identify underlying patterns of what worked and what didn't. For years, this was nothing more than a private document I'd revisit anytime my relationships were on the rocks.

But after helping so many men with this information, I realized that I had something really special to offer men who were experiencing one of the most painful chapters of their lives. And make no mistake, this is a chapter of your life that will pass. Keeping this all to myself just didn't seem right after seeing what kind of "advice" was available elsewhere.

Before we begin, I want to explain the purpose of this book and what you can expect.

First and most importantly, this book is designed to help you reclaim your power as a Grounded Man. A man who lives in alignment to his values and vision.

If you're anything like I was or like most men who come to me for help after a breakup, you may feel like you've lost your power as a man. And if you're being honest with yourself, you likely felt that way long before the breakup.

But now that your ex has moved on, this sense of powerlessness has reached its zenith. For the first time (maybe in years), you've realized how much your identity was wrapped up IN *her*. Without her, it's like someone blew a six-inch hole in your chest with a 50-caliber rifle; worse, you may have convinced yourself that she's the only one who can repair it.

The challenge men face is as simple as it is painful. When they're in this place of scarcity and desperation, it's impossible to thrive in life. It's even more difficult to have any chance of re-sparking attraction with your ex or another woman.

Until you reclaim your rightful role as the king of your own life and own your power, none of the strategies I'll share in this book will work. If you're operating from a place of scarcity and fear of ending up alone or needing your ex back in your life in order to feel whole and happy, you're doomed from the start.

Therefore, regaining your power—regardless of what happens between you and your ex—is the first and most important step on this journey.

I'm going to show you a roadmap for not only curing the pain, rejection, and abandonment you're feeling right now, but how to embark on the path to reclaiming your personal power.

Next, I'll show you how to identify the underlying patterns and behaviors that led to your breakup in the first place (and make sure you break these patterns for good).

I have to share a very simple truth with you: your breakup happened for a reason—even if you can't see it right now.

Breakups don't simply happen out of nowhere. There is a cause and effect dynamic at play. It might be unattractive behaviors, values misalignment, ignoring needs, taking her for granted, becoming complacent, or a combination of all these things built up and unaddressed overtime.

Once you start to recognize these patterns, you'll realize that they were likely at the heart of *previous* breakups, too. The problem is that most men go through life with low levels of self-awareness and blame their partners without looking in the mirror to identify their contributions to the break up.

But until you take responsibility then put in the work to *resolve* these patterns and behaviors, you'll remain stuck on the hamster wheel of romantic death. You'll fall in love, think you've found "the one," and then lose her all over again.

Whether it's in the next iteration of your relationship with your ex or a new relationship altogether, these mistakes will continue to sabotage your romantic life until you become aware of them and take action to fix them.

Now, the last thing I want to do is burden you with even more guilt for the way you may have acted or how you showed up in the relationship. But if you want to experience lasting change you have to come out of hiding and face it head on. I need to show you exactly where things went wrong, why they went wrong, and how you can correct them for good.

Once you understand the fundamental principles underlying every breakup or nasty divorce, you can leverage those principles to ensure that you never experience that type of torment again.

Finally, I'll share the exact steps you can take to re-attract your ex back into your life–and help you decide if this is *actually* what is best for your future.

You might not believe this, but many of the men who've gone through this process before have decided *not* to get back with their ex.

Yes, even though they began this journey by dreaming and begging for a path to get her back, crying at night and making desperate appeals to the universe to give them "just one more chance," they came to realize they were better off without her and were capable of so much better once they regained their power.

The ironic part? They made this decision even when they had the opportunity, even when they followed my strategies and *she* came back to *them*. By doing the work in this book, they realized that the relationship they once would have killed for no longer served the man.

This realization allowed them to walk away from *her* with their dignity and respect intact as they began the next chapter of a glorious life. When a man holds this frame, deciding for himself, "I don't need her to be happy and thriving," he has shifted out of scarcity and into his power… that's the place you'll soon be.

The truth is, I don't know your ex, and I don't know if getting back together is the right thing to do or not. I can't give you direct answers, but I *can* guide you on the journey to discovering them for yourself. I can help you as you make decisions that will benefit you in the future, and my expertise comes from years of experience in helping men in this exact situation.

My goal is simply to give you two options:

1. **To reclaim your power, recover faster, and set you up for success in a new relationship.**
   You'll have to decide for *yourself* that you no longer want to be in your past relationship. This will open you up to exciting new options, possibilities, and journeys to explore.

   Or…

2. **To re-attract your ex and co-create a new relationship together.**
   The process outlined in this book will give you the best chance of attracting your ex back into your life. You'll learn how to leverage psychological "attraction triggers" that defy her expectations and create a rapid emotional shift inside her. This shift can transform her attitude from cold and distant to reminiscing about the positive memories you shared and reaching out to you.

The option here is *not* to simply "get back together," but for you to experience a personal transformation in the way you show up to life and relationships. This will give you the opportunity to create a new relationship together that serves both of you. The choice is yours.

Ultimately, no matter how you feel right now, you may decide that the relationship you lost is worth fighting for—or it's not. Many of you reading this may *not* want to get back with your ex. You know that even though it hurts right now, the breakup was for the best.

Maybe you're simply looking for a guidebook to help you navigate your emotions and the pain of the experience, while potentially giving you the tools to recover and reestablish a friendly relationship with your ex (instead of the cold and chaotic person she may have morphed into when the relationship ended). Others may be unclear about whether or not they want to get their ex back, or simply have her return in a more open, loving way then later decide it's best to be friends.

Whether you're looking to heal from your breakup and recover faster, *or* you want to learn how to rekindle the attraction with your ex and reinvent your relationship so it can stand the test of time, I can promise you this: if you follow the framework outlined in this book, you *will* achieve the first outcome and have the best possible chance of realizing the second.

The journey begins.

HOW TO USE THIS BOOK

Most of the work that lies ahead is avoiding critical mistakes which only increase pain, push her away, and extend the breakup recovery period.

I can't stress this enough. Doing the right things matters, but avoiding the wrong things is even more important on this journey. As such, I want to be clear that even though you may be tempted to skip chapters or gloss over sections that don't seem to apply to you—*don't*.

Regardless of your goals during this process—whether you're trying to get back with your ex or move on and into a new relationship—the price of your mistakes is infinitely higher than the reward for the right actions.

I'm sharing from personal experience. I'm guilty of doing all the right things for months only to make one major mistake that erased all progress. Doing the right things is important, but avoiding the wrong actions is absolutely vital to your growth and success. Every mistake you make carries with it the pain of lost respect, relinquished power, and a fractured identity as a man. They lead to regret and humiliation as you waste months or even years of your life, wishing you could go back in time and undo the things you said or the way you acted.

Rest assured, each chapter will highlight the different pitfalls which most men fall into and how to avoid them. Just as importantly, I'll be sharing fundamental principles of human psychology, relationships, and attraction that will build on each other to help you create the transformation you're seeking. Without a clear understanding of the foundational ideas of this framework, later chapters won't be as effective as they could be.

So, my invitation is simple. Read through every chapter in sequence until the end, regardless of whether you want to move on or want to get your ex back. Then, most importantly, *take action.*

Remember, information without implementation is impotent and knowledge is only power when it's applied consistently. Take notes on the biggest lessons you learned and apply them. And I promise, you'll come out the other side of this journey stronger, more powerful, and more grounded than you ever thought possible.

WANT RESULTS FASTER?

You can learn more about the work I do with men at knowledgeformen.com/grow

CHAPTER 1:

CAN YOU HANDLE THE TRUTH?

THE CURSE OF CLOSURE

When a man is in the throes of a breakup, a single, soul-consuming question keeps repeating in his mind: *"Why?"*

"Why" takes on many different forms. Why is this happening after everything I did? Why did she leave me even though everything seemed to be going well? Why didn't she tell me how she was feeling so I could have done something about it earlier? Why did she leave me for *him* despite everything we've shared together? Why wasn't I enough for her?

Breakups can cause even the strongest man to feel lost, abandoned, rejected, and unworthy. Friends often try to downplay this pain with pithy platitudes, like, "There are plenty of other fish in the sea." But the fact remains that breakups are psychologically and emotionally devastating. This kind of emotional hurt has been proven, to the point that MRI scans show our post-breakup brains triggering the same pain pathways as a broken bone or third-degree burn.

To make sense of this pain, most men seek closure. They chase a fool's hope that if she says the right words or tells them what they want to hear, the pain will lessen, and they'll finally move on with their lives. Or worse, they cling to the idea that they can interrogate her to the point where she'll reveal the *true* cause of the breakup, and thus present the man with the opportunity to fix it and win her back.

But inside of this frantic questioning lies a hidden problem.

THE PITFALL OF THE CLOSURE CONVERSATION

You must make peace with not knowing *why* things happened the way they did. I want to make it clear that you cannot get closure from your ex… *yet*.

The reason is simple. She can't give you closure because she doesn't have closure yet herself. She may not know the true reason she broke up with you or why the relationship lost its spark. Even if she does, she's unlikely to share her feelings because she knows that it would only cut a deeper wound or create more conflict. No matter how deeply you want it, you must accept that giving you closure is not in *her* best interest. It prolongs the pain for both of you and fuels an often-false hope that you can win her back delaying your recovery.

This means that almost any answers she gives you will either be untrue or incomplete. It's not because she's malicious or deceptive, but because the process of a breakup is inherently emotional, confusing, and agonizing—even if *she* broke up with you and seems content with her decision.

She is likely unaware of the true patterns, behaviors, and problems that caused her feelings to change. The only thing she knows is that she doesn't want to be in a relationship with you right now. That's a truth she may have been mulling over for months, agonizing with herself over the "what ifs" and the "maybes." She's likely been talking with her friends and family to feel validated in her decision. She also may have been making dozens of thinly veiled attempts to fix the problem on her own, attempts that were either unrecognized or unrequited by you.

But now? She's finally gathered the courage to end the relationship. It doesn't matter if there are "valid" reasons that make sense to you or not. You can't find flaws in her "logic" that will magically change her mind because her decision isn't logical, at least not entirely. It's emotionally driven. She feels that this is the right decision for her at this moment.

But how can she explain this to you? How can she look the man she loved in the eyes and say, "I don't love you anymore"? How can she make you understand that she doesn't have a definite reason for leaving, that she's just as confused and hurt as you are, even though her pain is easier to bear because she's been processing it for months?

She can't. And she won't. Instead, she'll give you a laundry list of trite explanations that veil the ugly truth. These explanations will either give you nothing to hold onto—because they don't make sense logically—or mislead you, causing you to lose sleep imagining all the things you could have done differently in the past.

You might hear things like:

- I'm not ready for a serious relationship.
- I need to focus on myself, and you should too.
- I need to focus on my career and where I'm going in life.
- I need to explore other "options" and get this out of my system.
- I'm not sure what I want and it's not fair to drag you along.
- I feel like we're going in different directions.
- I love you, but I'm not in love with you anymore.

And the list goes on. But all of these things are code for one brutal truth: *I don't want to be in this relationship anymore.* But there's another layer to this conversation that most men miss.

If you want to get back with your ex, closure is a subtle but lethal form of self-sabotage.

By attempting to get closure and desperately trying to make sense of why the relationship ended, you put her in a position where she's forced to logically dig through the past and identify every flaw about you and the relationship. That's going to have the opposite effect; it's going to bolster her decision that there were many problems and challenges, ones that she may have otherwise ignored.

The more you ask her "why," the more she'll be pressured to come up with reasons that alleviate your frustration. That will only mean more reasons she can point to for why she broke up with you. It will just reinforce her decision and make her feel validated in her decision to break up.

Seeking repeated closure subjects you and your relationship to a death by a thousand cuts. With each text, call, or interaction, you're pushing her further away and creating more distance between you and her. As painful as it is, the best thing you can do for yourself, for her, and if you desire a future with her is to make peace with not knowing her exact reasons because it doesn't make a difference in the present moment.

> **By allowing the relationship to end without closure, it creates a sense of mystery in her mind. She'll question if she made the right decision to end the relationship and struggle to know exactly why she did.**

When friends and family ask her why she broke up with you, she'll be more likely to feel uncertain and confused by her decision instead of having a prepared laundry list of your every fault and failure. Her own lack of clarity leads her to wonder, "Did I make the right decision?"

When she's operating from this mind frame, those closest to her will be less likely to vilify you. Assuming that you treated her well and didn't give her an obvious reason to leave (i.e., infidelity or abuse), this dynamic can cause her friends and family to become your undercover allies. They'll remind her of the good times the two of you shared, the value you provided, and the way you made her life better. They may be people who support her in reaching out and working through the problems you experienced.

However, when you attempt to force closure in a high stakes debate, the situation reverses. She becomes painfully aware of everything that was wrong with the relationship, often creating and exaggerating problems in her mind that weren't that big of a deal, before unleashing a barrage of logical justifications to the people around her. The litany of well-formed complaints can cause them to rally around her like white knights and reinforce her belief that she's better off without you. Even worse, because their experience of you is likely limited to brief interactions and whatever *she* has told them, they'll be more likely to discourage her when she does feel the urge to reach out and reconnect. Instead of having allies, your bid for closure will turn the important people in her life into your enemies, creating an uphill battle that makes the journey more challenging.

She knows how she *felt,* and she likely has valid reasons for how she *feels* right now. But when you respect her decision and move on gracefully without fighting tooth and nail, it creates unresolved tension inside of her experience. If she isn't being forced to revisit the relationship's problems logically and repeatedly, she may begin to doubt if she made the right decision.

And from that seed of doubt springs the opportunity for her to reflect on the relationship in a more positive light. It can lead to a desire to resolve the uncertainty of why the relationship ended, and in many cases, spark a desire to reconnect with you.

But for this to happen, you must first understand why the relationship *actually* ended.

THE TRUTH ABOUT WHY SHE LEFT

The real reason your relationship ended is simple:

She lost attraction and an emotional connection to you.

Every other reason she's shared or idea you've thought of ultimately leads back to this truth. If she *wanted* to be with you right now, she would. But she doesn't. And it isn't because you left the toilet lid up, upset her over dinner last month or didn't get her the gift she wanted on her birthday. It's because somewhere in the course of your relationship—likely in the last twenty percent of the time you were together—you stopped showing up as the man she fell in love with. So, she stopped feeling the love, connection, and sexual polarity that attracted her to you in the first place.

When a woman feels high levels of attraction for a man, it overrides any logical reasons she might have for wanting to break up or look for problems within a relationship. It motivates her to show up, keep you happy, and work on issues by eliminating the doubts and "what ifs."

- Low attraction = low motivation to work on relationship and overcome issues
- High attraction = high motivation to work on relationship and overcome issues

Later in this book, I'll break down the difference between attractive and unattractive behavior in detail to help you spot the patterns and problems that caused her to lose attraction to you. But first you must understand the most fundamental principle or "equation" that controls every relationship.

THE RELATIONSHIP EQUATION

Even though relationships often seem complex and random by nature, at a fundamental level, they are elegantly simple and predictable. Your success or failure in a relationship hinges on your understanding of one foundational concept. Specifically, you must understand the implicit value exchange of relationships which can be summarized by asking two simple questions:

"Am I getting more out of this relationship than I'm putting into it? And can I get a greater return from a different partner?"

While it might seem unfair to diminish relationships by comparing them to financial investments, the truth is that they aren't all that different. More importantly, they illustrate the underlying value exchange of relationships in a way that is easy to understand.

If you invest \$1,000 and consistently turn it into \$2,000, you would never *stop* putting money toward that investment. However, if you *lost* money, you would quickly stop investing and move your money somewhere else where you can get a better return.

This same principle holds true in relationships. The reason that a person stays in a relationship, whether it's platonic or romantic, is that the relationship gives equal or greater value than it takes. Whenever this dynamic is broken, then one or both individuals withdraw since they feel they're losing and could do better elsewhere.

For example, we've all had those friends who simply stopped providing value at some point in the relationship. They stopped growing and progressing in their own lives and no longer offered anything interesting to us. The value of our shared history together may have kept the friendship holding on by a thread, but eventually, the cost of the relationship became too high. It caused us to cut ties and find new, more valuable sources of connection.

This is the same process that unfolded in your relationship with your ex. Whether you were consciously aware of it or not, you stopped offering her value equal or greater to the value you needed from her. When a man provides less value than what she believes she's worth, a woman loses attraction to him and begins to explore elsewhere to get the value she believes she's worth. She will eventually choose what is best for herself.

High levels of attraction are a byproduct of high levels of value, perceived or real. The more valuable you are to her as a man, the more attraction she will feel, and the more she will fight to make the relationship work, regardless of any obstacles.

But this concept of value goes well beyond the amount of money you make, the horsepower of your car, or the number of square feet in your house. That's why it's important to understand this next part.

THE SOURCE OF VALUE & ATTRACTION

After reading the last section and understanding that the main reason she left is that she lost attraction, the obvious question you should be asking yourself is:

How do I increase my attraction?

Simple. You increase attraction by increasing your value and decreasing your neediness.

Attraction = Value - Neediness

To put this in easy financial terms for understanding, imagine your relationship is like a bank account. When you break up or are close to a breakup, you're in a form of relationship debt. And just like financial debt, there are a few ways to escape from relationship debt.

1. You either increase your value (income)
2. Decrease your neediness (spending)
3. Do both

In other words, you were failing to meet her needs (value decreased), yet you still expected *her* to meet *your* needs (neediness increased). Over time, this became an exhausting dynamic that led to the loss of attraction and eventually, the breakup.

We'll explore exactly what it looks like to increase your value later in this book and give more detailed examples, yet during a breakup start by decreasing neediness. During a break up, this is where the most pain, devastation, and regret comes from and it's what pushes her away, sometimes for good.

Our goal right now is to stop the bleeding. In the next chapter, I'm going to show you how to do this *practically*. What you're going to learn will be in direct opposition to your natural instincts, what your peers are telling you and defy what you know about love and attraction.

BIG IDEAS:

1. **Seeking closure works against you.**

    As much as you may want it, you cannot get closure from her. Emotions are too high for any valuable truths to be revealed early on. Pressuring your ex for closure will only reinforce her decision to leave, validate her negative feelings, and create a bigger defensive wall against you.

2. **Attraction is determined by a simple formula, "Value - Neediness = Attraction"**

    Relationships are predicated on a mutual value exchange. The reason to stay in a relationship is because it offers equal or greater value than it takes. When you provide less value and take her for granted, you begin losing her attraction.

3. **Your relationship ended because you stopped being attractive to your partner.**

    Once attraction has fallen, small issues become big issues and there is no motivation to "work" on the relationship. The good news is, once you understand this foundational principle, it gives you a greater sense of power—whether your goal is to reinvent your last relationship or move on into a new one.

CHAPTER 2:

THE FOG OF REALITY

MISMATCHED TIMELINES

While society tends to diminish the pain that men experience after a romantic separation, the truth is that breakups are just as devastating for men as they are for women. According to many studies, they're more devastating.

Men experience longer and greater levels of psychological distress than women and—adding insult to injury—our struggle is often demeaned or ignored altogether. Despite the intensity of the pain we experience, we're told by society to simply "toughen up," "get over her," "go have sex with more women" and "just move on." We have few strong support systems, little guidance, and often no one who gives a damn because as men, we're supposed to be able to just handle it on our own and "walk it off."

When this cultural attitude toward the male experience is combined with the biological and psychological pain of a breakup, men find themselves treading in dangerous waters. Because of the pain we experience—again, which is processed by the brain in the same way as a broken bone—our levels of the "feel good" neurotransmitters dopamine, serotonin, and oxytocin plummet. The stress hormones cortisol and adrenaline spike.

On a biological level, we're like a junkie coming down from a high. One of our primary sources of positive emotions and "happy chemicals" was stripped away unexpectedly. The shock thrusts us into a brutal "fight or flight" cycle with no one to fight or flee from. Just like the junkie, we'll unknowingly engage in weak, regretful and embarrassing behaviors to get our fix from her. All of this makes the situation worse.

But there's an even deeper, more damaging problem lurking in this experience. In most breakups—specifically where the woman leaves the man—the pain seems one-sided. You're reeling with shock, feeling like someone just ripped open your chest, asking yourself, "How is this happening?"

But her? She seems calm, certain, and confident in her decision, acting like a completely different person. It looks like she's casually plucking out the pieces of your soul like petals from a flower. Not only could she appear unphased by the breakup, she may even seem excited. She's embarking on a new adventure and leaving you to bleed out in the dust behind her. It's enough to make you question whether any of the emotions, love, or experiences you shared were actually "real."

If you were an addict, she's the dealer. And even though she has the very thing that could ease your pain and make you feel alive again, she's refusing to give it to you, no matter what you offer, how much you're willing to change, how good you are at debating, or how much you beg and plead.

The pain of the breakup coupled with her apparent lack of remorse is enough to drive any man absolutely mad. So, before we can explore the path ahead of you and give you the tools to navigate this new journey ahead of you, it's important for us to take a step back and bridge the gap between where *you* are and where *she* is. Whether you're trying to get her back or not, for the sake of your own sanity, you need to understand why there's such a deep divide between your respective experiences.

The difference between your experience and her experience is driven primarily by a mismatch in timelines.

She's been mulling over her decision for some time. She's likely been talking with her friends and family, thinking, debating, agonizing over whether or not she wants to stay with you. Depending on how long the two of you were together, she spent months or even years processing her decision, contemplating different outcomes, and emotionally distancing herself. You probably felt this as she was showing up less and less for you during this time.

She may have dropped hints about important issues. She might have gently (or not so gently) nudged you to take different actions. It's possible she even explicitly addressed the problems. But for one reason or another, you failed to understand the brevity of what was being shared when her emotional attraction for you was high enough to actually work on the issues.

You may have known that something was wrong, or you may not of. But chances are, you didn't know *how* wrong they were until the moment the hammer fell. This is where the disconnect becomes your Achilles' heel.

She's been preparing for this big conversation. She's worked through all of her reasons and arguments with her friends and family and even rehearsed what she was going to say for days leading up to it. With her level of preparation comes an equal level of commitment and certainty to move forward with it.

She's made her decision and decided to see it through to the end. She's already ascended the various stages of grief and reached a place of acceptance with her decision. Even though it was likely just as hard for her in the beginning as it is for you now, she processed her decision emotionally *before* bringing it to you.

To make matters worse, she will likely have an easier time after the breakup because there may be other men on standby, circling like vultures and waiting for her to be single. The second she starts removing photos of you from her social media or changes her relationship status, her DMs will be flooded, all of them boosting her ego, getting her excited, and validating her choice. Even if this isn't the case, she can easily open any dating app, start swiping, and find men eager to go out with her.

You, on the other hand, were likely blindsided. Instead of having months to think things through, rehearse your conversations, and create plans for how you were going to live your life as a newly single man, you woke up one morning in a committed relationship but went to bed that night alone, shocked and devastated. You're trapped in the early stages of grief, grappling with the sudden loss of a lover.

And unlike her, you likely don't have a sea of new options waiting to be explored. Even the most attractive and high-status men can have less power in the dating game than the average woman. You likely don't have a string of women sliding into your DMs or the ability to "swipe" your way into a new romance within a few days. You're alone… and it only makes the experience that much more painful.

Regardless of her intentions, she just put you through a psychological ambush. She had time to muster reinforcements, plan her attack, and execute. She even knew what she would do afterward. You, on the other hand, were caught with your guard down. You were just a good soldier, sleeping peacefully in your tent, not knowing that your world was about to change overnight.

And just like a military ambush, your gut instinct is to fight fire with fire, to sound the alarm and rush to face the enemy head on with an onslaught of logical arguments and pleas. But the problem is, the tools at your disposal won't work against her defenses. Because right now, your only line of defense is literally the past you had together. It's nothing but memories of the good times you had, the experiences you shared, the love you experienced. You'll be tempted to use these memories and times she said "I love you" as a proverbial bargaining chip, begging her to look back and remember that what you had is worth fighting for.

But from all of the deliberation and confusion she's gone through, she's made up her mind—and no matter how hard you fight to win her back with logic, you aren't going to change her mind in that moment.

Even if she's able to point to logical reasons for her decision, the truth is that they don't hold as much weight as she is making you believe. While these logical justifications may have played a role in her departure, she left because she lost attraction. Your value diminished in her eyes and she lost the emotional connection that once glued your relationship together. She has no reason to stay because she no longer *feels* what she needs to feel to stay in the relationship and make things work.

But it's unlikely that she is consciously aware of this and even less likely that she'll explicitly share this. Instead, she'll share logical reasons that seem superficial and might not make any sense or point to insignificant or even non-existent problems to try and help you understand what's happening. It's not because she's wicked or malicious, but because she's trying to make this as easy as possible for both of you.

But what most women might not understand is that these logical assaults only serve to fuel a false hope for their partners. After all, if there's a logical problem, it only goes to follow that there must be a logical solution and that's an area where men thrive. But even if you were able to resolve every grievance she shared with the wave of a hand, it wouldn't change how she feels emotionally about you in this moment. Right now, the attraction is at an all-time low, and solving the surface layer issues—even if they contributed to her loss of attraction—won't change how she feels.

The gut-wrenching truth is there's nothing you can do right now to change her mind.

The harder you try, the more your value decreases and the more confident she becomes about moving forward without you. Begging, pleading, and negotiating will only serve to validate her feelings and further reduce your value and status in her eyes. The only option you have is to retreat and live to fight another day. Give her space to process what happened while you accept that you can't win her back… right now. Even if you aren't trying to win her back, any actions you take from a frame of trying to save the relationship (e.g. staying friends, opening up the relationship to new partners, offering to buy her anything) will only reduce your value in her eyes.

This might be one of the hardest things you ever have to do, but whether you want to get her back or simply move on with your life, you must accept her decision and walk away calmly. Any actions you take to try and win her back from your current state of desperation will only undermine your value further and make the pain of recovery that much harder.

WHY SHE WON'T COME BACK (YET)

We've covered the most basic truths about your situation. Your ex left you because she lost emotional attraction. And the reason she lost attraction is because you stopped providing greater value than you needed. Once you understand this, the solution becomes apparent.

Simply invert the equation. Increase your value, decrease your neediness, and become the type of man who can re-attract her.

But here's the catch. From your current state, you are incapable of attracting your ex because you are incapable of increasing your value at this time in her eyes. Worse, your weak state can often drive you to engage in humiliating, unattractive, and emasculating behaviors. Sadly, the stakes are at their highest when you are at your lowest point, namely, during the breakup conversation or immediately after it.

Attractive behaviors like accepting her decision with grace, respectfully moving on, and expressing gratitude for the times you shared, will intensify her emotional experience and may lead her to question her decision. They won't be sufficient to bring her back *yet*, but they can plant a seed of doubt that can grow into the idea of revisiting a connection with you in the future.

Inversely, unattractive behaviors like begging, pleading, bitterness, anger, name calling, emotional tantrums, logical arguments, and manipulation will be magnified, reinforcing her feelings and widening the gap between you. If you try to win her back from your current state, you'll plunge your "relationship account" into a deep and possibly insurmountable amount of relationship debt.

This is a crucial point: most women have been conditioned by previous relationships to expect unattractive and needy behaviors, especially during and post-breakup. She's *expecting* you to beg, plead, get angry, call her a "heartless bitch," or profess your undying love to her on your knees in tears... just like other men have in the past. She doesn't expect you to calmly respect her decision and walk away with your dignity intact. When you do, it will make her question her decision and wonder if she is making a mistake. Breaking the pattern of what is expected is an attraction trigger which can increase your value.

But it's up to you to accept that in this phase of the breakup, she's made her decision. Any action you take to oppose it will bring only drama, stress, and frustration, which will make the situation worse.

You need to re-engage from a place of power as a man, a sense of confidence in your ability to move forward with or without her.

ACCEPTING THE NEW REALITY

Once you understand the truth about where the two of you are in your respective timelines, regardless of what you want or how you feel, the next step is to accept your new reality. As of this moment, she is no longer your partner. Your role as her boyfriend, husband, or lover is over. With its ending, the dynamics you've grown accustomed to have ended, too.

The second she says, "It's over," your access and privilege of being her lover come to an end. As of this moment, you're just another guy who has a crush on her. As painful as this frame is to accept, you need to filter every action you take through this lens:

How would she react to a man she just met who acted this way?

To help you understand this better simply reverse the situation. How would you respond if a woman you just met called you ten times in a row, left a dozen lengthy and highly emotional texts and voice messages without you responding to any of them, showed up at your home or work unannounced at odd hours, or constantly begged you to commit to her when you've already said no? You'd avoid this person at all costs and that's exactly what she'll do to you if you act in a desperate way.

When you were committed lovers, you could expect her to be there for you through challenges. But that expectation does not exist anymore because you're *not* together, you're *not* lovers, and you're *not* her responsibility.

In the past, when you were down and emotional, she cared for you and offered her loving support. But now? These constant displays of intense emotional vulnerability are seen as weakness, proving to her that she made the right choice. She is no longer responsible for your emotions, your wants, or your needs. Any attempts that go against this will only repel her further.

She's made her decision, and it was a hard decision to make. It's her responsibility to follow through and own the choice she's made. The distance and cold behavior are also an attempt to protect *you*. She knows that the loving support you're craving will only fuel more confusion and pain on both sides.

She doesn't want to provide you with a false sense of hope or feel like she's leading you on by continuing to be emotionally available, loving, or supportive. As a result, her main line of defense is to shut herself off and shut you out, often by being very cold. Right now, from her current emotional state (which *can* change), engaging with you only pulls her back into the past, which she is trying to move on from.

So, during this phase, you must take complete and total ownership of your own emotions and experience. Expect nothing from her, ask nothing of her, and accept that she is not responsible for your pain, emotions, or recovery. Her emotions are hers. Your emotions are yours.

The inverse is also true. Any expectations she had of you must come to an end. If you were paying bills, running errands for her, fixing things for her, offering financial or professional support, or letting her use your car, that must also come to an end.

However, if there is a child in your relationship, you still have an obligation and the honor of continuing to meet that child's needs and wants. It is not a sign of weakness to continue doing everything you would normally do for your own children.

But between the two of you, your privileges as a lover have been revoked and so must hers. If you continue providing support for her that you wouldn't willingly provide to a woman you just met, it will decrease your value in her eyes. Cancel these favors and services calmly and gracefully.

Why? Because even though she's ceased providing her value to you as a lover, she still has power over you to get the "benefits" of being in a relationship *without* being committed to you and returning the favor. Why would she want to change this? She's free to date other men and gets all the perks of a supportive partner from you? Absolutely not.

And this is actually good news. The fact that your relationship ended in the first place shows that the past you're glorifying in your head probably isn't the full picture. There were problems you were and weren't aware of, patterns that didn't serve your growth, and areas where you weren't showing up as the man you needed to be. By understanding this and focusing on the future, you may have the opportunity to create a new relationship with her or with a new woman, and this new relationship can be free from these challenges now that you're aware of them.

To fully heal, process, recover, and open yourself up to the opportunity for reconciliation, you must treasure the lessons in front of you and stop holding onto the past as if it was a picture-perfect relationship. It wasn't.

Most importantly, you must do this *for yourself.* If you attempt to embark on this journey from a frame of neediness—thinking to yourself, "If I just follow these steps, she'll fall in love with me again and things will go back to the way they were"—not only will you do a disservice to yourself, but you'll sabotage any hope of salvaging the relationship. Any personal growth you undergo for the sole purpose of getting back with your ex will likely backfire because there has been no lasting change on the inside for yourself.

It's similar to the crash diets and obscure workouts people follow to get in shape for summer. When faced with the pain of displaying unsightly love handles and bulging beer guts for the world to see, it's relatively easy to feel motivated to hit the gym and say "no" to those free donuts at the office. But as soon as summer ends and the pain of embarrassment ends with it, they go right back to their old habits and patterns.

No positive change can be accomplished until you embrace your new reality with open eyes and a clear head on what's to come.

THE TWO PATHS AHEAD OF YOU

At this point, you now have two choices.

First, you can accept the new reality and understand where your ex is in her journey and where you are in your journey. You can acknowledge that there's nothing you can do to win her back *yet*.

Or you can fight it. You can let your biological and psychological impulses take the wheel, leading you to weak, needy, and unattractive behaviors that can push her away permanently.

And even if you logically understand everything I've laid out so far, there's still a part of you that's resisting the journey ahead. What your brain wants right now is a return to your former normal as quickly as possible. You lost connection, intimacy, regular access to sex and a source of potential children. Even if losing it was for the best, your brain wants to get it back at all costs!

My goal with this section is to equip you with an understanding of your options so you can resist your evolutionary impulses and keep the long game in mind. The decisions you make in the coming weeks and months will make all the difference, not only for the potential of a new relationship with your ex or a new partner but for your growth and power as a man.

At the heart of this decision is a simple question:

"What are the risks of each path and what are the rewards?"

If you choose to reject your new reality and fight against the breakup, what are the risks of this behavior? What are the rewards? Inversely, if you accept this new reality and commit to the process I'm going to outline in the coming pages, what are the risks and what are the rewards?

The good news is this question has already been answered. From my own personal experience and the experience of the thousands of men I've coached through this exact situation, I've witnessed the results of each path and the outcomes are always the same!

Regardless of how you feel or how convinced you may be that your situation is different, the fact is this: **Fighting reality offers a very**

low potential upside and a very high possible downside, leading to humiliation and an extended recovery process.

However, when we apply the question of risk versus reward to the path of accepting reality—giving your ex space, accepting her decision, and focusing on yourself, your growth, and your own life—the results will surprise you.

When you commit to your own growth and development as a man, you reclaim your power. You reflect and learn how you can show up better in relationships, reconnect with your core goals and social connections, and rebuild your foundation as a man from the ground up.

This leads to two possibilities. Either you transform yourself into a higher-value man and re-attract your ex from a place of power and abundance, or you learn from the experience, grow stronger, and go your separate ways. If it's the second option, you'll take the lessons you learned from your previous relationship to a new romance where you can start fresh with someone who's more in alignment with your values and vision.

Either way, you win. You will be a more attractive, stronger, and more grounded man because of what seems like a horrible experience today. And with many of the clients I coached through this process, many of the men who desperately wanted to get back with their ex later rejected her because they realized that they could experience an abundant dating life with women who were more compatible with their lives.

There's literally no downside to the path of acceptance and growth. You'll never look back on your life and wish that you'd been weaker, less powerful, or less attractive. And while you may worry that the path of acceptance will cause your ex to leave you for good or move on, you have to remember that she's already made the decision to breakup.

Once you understand the implicit risks and rewards of each path, the obvious question for you is: *"What do I do now?"*

And that's exactly what I'm going to share in the next chapter.

BIG IDEAS

1. **Understand Your Ex's Timeline**

   Your ex likely experienced just as much pain over the breakup as you did. The main difference is that she's on a different timeline. She processed the pain of her decision months ago, but you were blindsided when she shared that decision with you without warning.

2. **You Can't Win Your Ex Back from Your Current State**

   Your ex has lost attraction to you. And right now, there's no conversation, gift, or logical argument you can make to change that. Until you increase your attractiveness—which takes time apart and conscious effort—any drastic efforts you make right now will push her away.

3. **You Must Accept the New Reality**

   Your ex is no longer your partner or lover. She doesn't owe you anything and you don't owe her anything. If you try to fight this reality and win her back through manipulation, you will only reduce your attractiveness further and create a longer recovery process.

   If you do the opposite of what she expects by accepting this new reality, focusing inward, and thriving, then you stand the greatest chance of getting her back or moving on with your dignity and respect intact.

CHAPTER 3:

RECLAIMING YOUR POWER

WHAT SHE DOESN'T WANT YOU TO KNOW

No matter how certain she might seem about her decision when she broke up with you, she isn't always 100% sure she made the right decision. She still has doubts and questions that she hasn't yet answered. Assuming that your breakup wasn't caused by abuse or infidelity, the feelings your ex is experiencing can change if you operate effectively within this new reality.

The reality of single life rarely matches the fantasy she constructed in her head, especially since it's often influenced by others. Yes, she will experience a rush of newfound freedom, but as the weeks and months drag on, it may not be all that exciting. Maybe she's surrounding herself with people and activities that aren't really who she is, maybe the hangovers take a toll on her, maybe she finds herself alone at nights watching tv while glued to her phone. The thrill will die down much quicker if you give her space and allow her to experience life without you interfering. If this decision was the wrong one for her, she'll have to face that soon enough.

The challenge for you is that you won't see her true reality. Instead, you'll only see the social media highlight reel she wants people to see or what you hear from others. Remember, it took her months to make the decision to break up with you, so she has to commit to owning it. If you added value to her life while being a loving partner, chances are there are people who questioned her decision.

And she wants to prove to them—and to herself—that she was right.

When you *expect* her to post videos of parties, dates or social activities with people you've never seen before, you're less likely to fall into a weak, reactionary state where you do something that sabotages your value and all the progress you've made. When you can accept that this is a part of her process and it's supposed to happen, it allows you to remain calm and stay focused on your own journey—regardless of whether you want her back or not. She is doing what she is supposed to do and she's not losing her mind, even though it may appear that way.

When you accept her behavior as part of the process and understand that you're not necessarily seeing the full picture of her life, it becomes easier to navigate this phase from a grounded frame and maintain your power. Remember, her thoughts and emotions when she's alone at night before bed, in the early mornings, eating meals alone, when she's sitting in traffic… all of that is far different than what she portrays outwardly on social media.

That's why your behavior matters now more than ever. I cannot stress that enough. She's been conditioned by past breakups and relationships to expect certain behaviors and patterns from you, *the ex.* She's expecting you to act weak and needy, which will prove she was right in breaking up and make moving on even easier as you have now been labeled, the *crazy ex.*

Here's another possibility: she might be expecting you to remain a faithful "backup plan" waiting on standby and willing to take her back at a moment's notice. She doesn't expect you to have the power to move on, to grow into a stronger man, to accept her decision without trying to fix the mess. If you do, then what does that say about her value?

Is she not worth fighting for? Sometimes, the unusual behavior she posts on social media is an attempt to provoke a reaction from you to boost her ego and confirm you're still on standby. Even the sweetest of women unconsciously wants you to come running back to her, begging and pleading for another chance. It boosts her ego and proves to her how desirable she is during a time when she needs it most to validate her decision.

If you play into it by displaying needy behavior, offering support as if the breakup never happened, constantly contacting her, and continuing to show that you're waiting around for her while she enjoys the single life, it makes the breakup process easier on her and extremely hard on you.

When you're still trying to wedge yourself into her life, she doesn't have to face the full consequences of leaving you. Basically, she has no reason to change anything. But you must understand, no human is going to be happy with a side option... humans only want their best option. When you present yourself in a low-value way, you're encouraging her to keep searching for someone who is higher value.

But when the script flips and you reclaim your power as a man, owning your worth and value, her mind goes on a collision course with a new reality that she didn't anticipate. She expects you to be there for her, to give her the benefits of being in a relationship without the consequence of losing you, and to be at her beck and call because she thought she was more valuable and could do better. When this expectation is broken, it dismantles her vision and she loses control over the situation. It plants a seed of doubt in her mind about her decision to leave you.

Instead of having all the power, she realizes that she lost control of the situation. You aren't wrapped around her finger anymore and, in her mind, there's a real chance that she's lost a quality man who loved her... and it's all her fault. By virtue of human nature, this is an inherently uncomfortable position to be in. Humans seek to have control and certainty over their lives, not lack of control and certainty about the future.

The simple act of focusing inward and staying away speaks volumes. Whether your goal is to get her back or move on with your life, this principle is at the heart of the work we're going to do together.

THE REVERSAL OF POWER

To reclaim your sense of power and control and shift the emotional tide of your breakup, you must make a serious commitment to whether you want her back or want to move on. It won't be easy. It won't be comfortable. And during the early phases of the journey, you will be tempted to break this commitment time and time again. But as painful as it will be, it's the only path forward. It's the only approach that guarantees victory for you.

This commitment is simple. You must cease all contact with your ex.

I want to be clear. This is not a silly game or pickup strategy, this is what she asked for. She broke up with you. She declared that she wants to experience life without you, so the respectable response is to give her exactly what she wants and gracefully accept her request by withdrawing all communication.

After she decided to dismantle the relationship and leave you in pain, you don't owe her anything. She doesn't have the right to know what you're doing or how you're feeling. From the outside looking in, it should appear as if you've accepted her decision and are capable of moving on into a bright future.

As painful as it might be to accept, during this phase of the breakup, you also don't need to know how she's doing, what she's doing, or who she's doing it with. I know you want to alleviate your anxiety and are dying to know, but none of this will change your strategy moving forward, so it's best if you focus inward. Knowing those details by following her social media or asking about her through mutual friends will only derail you on this journey.

All of your attention and energy must be on your own life, your own growth, and what's in front of you in the present moment, not desperately holding onto the past that no longer exists. And every time you break this commitment—calling or texting her "just once," stalking her social media with third party accounts, or "accidentally" showing up to where she is—it slows your recovery and diminishes your value in her eyes, whether you want her back or not. This is not healthy and it's a recipe for an extended recovery process that will take way longer than it needs to.

> **I want to be clear that this commitment of ceasing contact is not indefinite. If *she* reaches out to you, I'm not encouraging you to ignore her.**

I'll explain how to handle this situation later in the book. But to fully capitalize on the opportunity to reinvent yourself, to become the type of man who is capable of not only reattracting his ex but attracting an even *higher*-quality woman if he desires, you must temporarily cease contact and shift your focus inward. This is why we spent so much time clarifying the mechanics of attraction and her expectations. It requires you to understand that she doesn't *want* to be in a romantic relationship with you right now, and that every attempt you make to subvert her desires only pushes her further away.

But here's the challenge: even if you can logically acknowledge and agree with everything I've laid out so far, you'll still be tempted to reach out, especially when you are feeling lonely. It's in your DNA.

Men want to solve problems and overcome challenges. Men want to take action and solve crises. But what I'm asking you to do right now when you are in a great deal of pain is one of the hardest things that a man can do: *nothing*.

From a biological standpoint, your brain is experiencing the same visceral reactions as you would if your ex was physically dying. If she was drowning in a river, you'd jump in to save her. And that's exactly what your brain *believes* is happening right now.

You're losing someone that you love. Your evolutionary hardwiring will propel you into action to solve the problem by any means necessary. In the same way, you become convinced that you that you must do something to gain her back and "save" the relationship from dying.

But as magnificent as your brain is, it doesn't understand the psychological journey she's experiencing or the dynamics of attraction in the 21st century. It doesn't realize that any action you take to get her back during or immediately following the breakup only serves to boost her ego and distances you further from her.

Many of you reading this might want your ex back more than you want to breathe. You'd do *anything* to get her back. If she called you tomorrow and told you she would only get back with you if you walk barefoot across a football field of broken glass, you'd happily do it. Well, here you go. Here is that tough challenge.

Seize contact with your ex and commit to your own growth for the time being.

I know that this is hard to accept. And I know from personal experience—from several devastating breakups of my own—that it's even harder to actually do for weeks and months. Because right now, you're experiencing an all-out internal psychological onslaught, yet the first step to reclaim control of your life is to accept reality. When you cease contact and consciously choose to let go of your ex for a period of time, remain calm and focus inward, you are beginning to turn the chaos into a season growth.

By fully committing to this process, it can create a psychological reversal where *she* begins to experience the same emotions currently wreaking havoc on your mind. It can foster feelings of anxiety and fear at the thought of losing a man she loved forever. When you navigate this journey correctly, her worry can compound to the point where she takes action and reaches out (I'll show you how to increase the chances of this happening throughout this book).

You can't lose in this scenario. No matter what happens, the outcome will still be in your favor. You'll either get her back, or you'll grow into the type of man who's capable of attracting a higher-quality woman who's a better fit for your life. Both outcomes are wins.

Now that you understand the foundational principle of the work ahead, I want to explain how following this principle will impact her mind. It's the reason why, respecting her decision and giving her space is the most effective strategy moving forward.

LET HER PSYCHOLOGY DO THE HEAVY LIFTING

Note to the reader: While some of the following sections will apply primarily for men looking to get their ex back, there are still powerful lessons to be learned even if you aren't interested in pursuing your ex any further. One of the foundational themes you'll find in this book is that emotions do change. This is true for her, and it's true for you.

Your emotions are in a heightened state and you may believe that you don't want her back because of the anger, confusion and pain you're experiencing right now. Your ego may be influencing this decision to move on quickly and replace your ex with a better partner to prove your worth. This may be true now, but after you've had space and time alone to reflect, this could change.

You may decide that you're ready to move on or you may not. But when you better understand what's happening between the two of you, you'll be in the best position to choose what you want, regardless of how your feelings change with time.

*　　*　　*

When you fully embrace the reversal of power and deny her any more attention, chasing, and ego-boosting validation after the breakup, it shifts her psychological experience. During the initial stages of the breakup, you were the one experiencing fear, loss, abandonment, and separation anxiety. After all, *she* was the one making the decision to leave you.

But often, her decision carried with it certain expectations and assumptions about your behavior following the breakup. She expects this to be an easy transition because she thinks she has you as a fallback option. Even though she's rescinded her love and affection from you, she expects you to continue providing value for her—even if it's only through the validation you give her by continuing to be in her life. She *expects* you to be waiting for her, to be available at a moment's notice, to even beg and plead, to put her on a pedestal while she enjoys all of the fun and freedom of being a single woman.

But when you deny her this expectation by respecting her decision and removing yourself from her life, it challenges the assumptions she had about her post-breakup life. The human brain is good at making predictions about what will or won't happen, and it *hates* when its predictions are wrong.

When she left, she thought her value was higher than yours. Period. She felt that she could do better—and decided that she *would* do better. By staying in her life and chasing her, you prove her prediction correct and no further thought or action on her part is necessary. But when you disappear? It creates dissonance in her mind, causing confusion, curiosity, mystery about you, and uncertainty.

Instead of thinking, "I want to try this single life out and I can always get him back if I don't like it," the prediction is broken. She's forced to experience the full consequences of her decision and live in a reality where she's lost someone she loved and who loved her dearly.

The anxiety that she will experience as she sits alone with this reality is a powerful precursor to attraction. Removing yourself from her life creates scarcity, and just like in economics, scarcity increases value. The reason we're willing to pay more for goods is because the demand for those goods is greater than the supply. A bottle of water at a grocery store is pennies versus at a festival in the desert where it can cost $10.

When you apply this same principle to the dynamics of a breakup, it's easy to see why this process of reversing power is effective in increasing one's value. Every time you contact, chase, or pursue her, it shows that you're still available to her and that her initial prediction was correct. Post breakup when your partner has a surplus of your time, attention, and affection that's always available to her it becomes less valuable. But when you eliminate the supply of your time, attention, and affection altogether, your value increases.

Initially, she held the power in breaking up with you. But you hold the power in walking away and giving her exactly what she wants—a life without you while you thrive without her. She will lose the man she fell in love with, a man with whom she shared countless positive experiences, brought to friends' and family gatherings, bared the depths of her soul and body to, and overcame struggles with.

Remember, the feelings and emotions she had for you haven't vanished, although it feels like it. They're being suppressed beneath a defensive wall that demands change. Attachment runs deep in the human psyche. Assuming that the relationship was mostly positive, she is *still* attached to you, even if she won't admit it to you or even herself. But until you remove yourself from her life completely, she'll never experience the complete loss of that attachment and the full impact of her decision.

The problem is, most men are unable to remove themselves from their exes' lives post-breakup for any meaningful length of time. They try for a few days or a few weeks then succumb to their natural psychological impulses to solve the problem and chase her, smothering her when her defenses are at her highest. They never allow her the space and time to miss them, forcing her to reject the man repeatedly, which strengthens her prediction that she was right after all. But for her to reevaluate her decision, she must fully experience what she thinks she wants and be given the time and space to wonder, "Did I do the right thing?"

Trust that human nature and her own psychology are far more effective tools at changing her emotions and increasing your value than any action you can take post-breakup. For anything meaningful to happen between the two of you, she must arrive at the conclusion that she wants to reconnect independently of anything you say or do. Logical coercion and emotional manipulation may bring her back physically for a short time. But until her emotions change organically on her own, there can be no lasting or worthwhile reconciliation.

Assuming that you had a good relationship—you were a good partner who treated her well, there was no infidelity or abuse, and you had more positive moments than bad—the act of ceasing contact can elicit a strong, unexpected response from her.

Human beings are hardwired with what psychologists call "loss aversion bias." It means that we will work harder to avoid losing something that we have than we will in order to gain something new. For example, when you lose your phone that you've had for years all you want is to find your phone and you are less interested in buying a new and better phone.

This is exactly why the act of ceasing contact post breakup is so effective. It's painful to accept, but the man you are right now is the man that she lost attraction for. In this moment, you are the man she fell *out* of love with. Every interaction you have during the weeks and months immediately following the breakup will come from this weak frame.

But you weren't always that man. There are deep, powerful memories of the man she fell in love with, the man she shared her mind, body, and soul with for an extended period of time. But that version of you exists only in her mind. The attractive version of you—at least until you complete this journey—is in the past.

By removing yourself for a period of time, you allow her to reminisce about the times you shared together, about the attractive man you were. Trust that she loved you for a reason, that she stayed with you for as long as she did for a reason, that she happily introduced you to her friends and family for a reason. That she was physically, emotionally and spiritually intimate with you for a reason. Believe that she will slowly start to remember those reasons with enough time and space.

Fully committing to this journey is not easy. It's painful, gut wrenching, and emotionally draining at times. But it's an effective path to creating more attraction, increasing your value, and triggering her to have a change of heart about the breakup and, in many cases, reconnecting with you. When you understand the psychological mechanisms at play, it's easier to stay strong when temptation arises. It's easier to keep yourself grounded as challenges arise—and arise they will!

Now that you understand the foundational concepts of reversing the power dynamic after the breakup, I want to briefly address some of the common questions men have regarding this process and what to expect.

What are the chances she reaches out because she wants to rekindle?
The truth is, I don't know. There are no guarantees in life. However, I *do* know from my own experience and my experience coaching men that the strategy in this book is the best shot you have at getting her back.

Remember, weak and needy behavior is *guaranteed* to push her further away and cause you to suffer more from an extended recovery period. Committing to the reversal of power and ceasing contact will lead to two outcomes: you either get her back or you reclaim your power faster so you can move forward into a new relationship. The chances of success with this strategy are 100%. But that doesn't mean that success is guaranteed to look exactly like you want it to in this moment.

I can say that roughly 50% of the men who follow this strategy are able to re-connect with their exes and get another chance at the relationship, but only if there is change from both parties to resolve what led to the breakup in the first place. If you follow this game plan and your relationship wasn't troubled by abuse or infidelity, I've seen it happen many times.

But regardless of the outcome, you will win. Either you will get her back, or you will move forward with someone who is more aligned with your values and vision. Either option should excite you for the future.

What if she goes out with other men?
One of the hardest parts of the breakup process isn't just losing your partner, it's the feeling of losing your partner to another man. It's especially hard when she starts dating other men quickly after leaving you. Even though this experience is something you don't want to hear, it can work to your advantage. Let me explain.

First, you must acknowledge that you are no longer her lover. The relationship has ended, and she has every right to date and experience anyone she wants, as do you. One *very* dangerous thing you can do when going through a breakup is to frantically reach out in anger, heavy emotion or extreme jealousy when you find out that she's going out with other men or hear that she's already dating someone new.

Everything can be going well for you post-breakup. You may even be dating new women yourself and feeling like you've fully accepted the situation. But the second a new man enters her life, and you see her smiling and being held by someone new? Your emotions can become highly triggered as you sense a loss of control again. Rage, self-sabotage, and frantic behaviors you didn't even know you were capable of can come rushing to the surface. If this happens, you must stay grounded and remain calm despite the intense dark feelings you may experience. Breathe. Hit the gym. Connect with supportive friends and family. Do not unleash emotional tantrums via phone, text or social media towards your ex or physically confront the other man with aggression. Instead, let the other men do this.

Not only will you undo any progress you've already made, but your weak, needy behavior will be a huge contrast to her new lover's more attractive behaviors. Any attempts to get back with her at this time will actually make her have stronger emotions for the new man. Your needy behavior makes him seem more valuable and desirable since she can compare both of you. One is weak, stressful, and angry, the other is more fun, carefree, and attractive. Women will always move towards their highest value option and treat their lowest value options poorly.

However, if you hold strong to your commitment and allow her to have her experiences without interfering with her life, the opposite reaction often occurs. Now that you've given her room to reminisce about the man she fell in love with—your past self—she'll be comparing every new man she meets to who you were in the past.

Remember, attachment runs deep on the subconscious level. You have a shared history and plethora of positive experiences that other new men don't. You knew her body and mind in a way that they can't possibly know in such a short amount of time. You knew her wants, fears, dreams, and quirks in a way that will take them years to understand.

By remaining in a grounded frame and avoiding emotionally reactive fits of anger, jealousy, or neediness, you'll project strength. That creates space for the other men in her life to make mistakes and show needy behavior which she can contrast with you. After a breakup, she'll likely be emotionally unavailable and distant about becoming too intimate with someone new so soon. She's likely looking for a rebound to cope with the pain of her own loss and loneliness, not a life partner. By allowing other men to chase her and put her on a pedestal, you appear stronger and they appear weaker.

You must be unaffected by other new men that enter her life. You must maintain a mind frame that you are the prize, king and high value man, and she can try her best to search for another man. She's expecting that the other men she's dating will elicit an emotional reaction from you. When it doesn't? The mystery and confusion she feels about you will intensify and she'll be pulled into these positive memories of you. What does this say about her value and yours?

Trust that what you shared together was *real*. No matter how she's acting post breakup, she did love you. By experiencing other men who will likely showcase needy behaviors as she is emotionally unavailable, she'll start to remember your love, affection, and value.

What if she reaches out?

Do not ignore her if your goal is to get her back. As you go through this process, you should expect her to test you. Do not respond in an overly emotional way or with a lot of excitement. Do not pour out your emotions and talk about how much you've missed her so quickly. It's a trap. This is what she wants, and she may not even respond to that type of heavy emotional response from you. She just wants to know that you're still on standby. Shortly after you commit to this process, it's possible that she'll reach out and attempt to connect, which presents a unique challenge for men.

Even though it's a positive sign if she reaches out to you, that goal comes with some conditions.

Indeed, *you* are in a better position as *she* is reaching out to you. Maybe it's in a text, a social media message, a call, or email. A social media "like" or an random comment on a photo or video does not mean you should fervently reach out to her and put your emotions on the table. You need to hold out for a direct private message, text, or phone call.

I can assure you, that these little "notice me" gestures such as liking your post are a test. The challenge for many men is that they will misinterpret her little tests for invitations to reconcile.

If you feel the need to reply, then take your time, respond respectfully, politely, and with some aloofness. Make it shorter than her message, then let it be and carry on.

It helps for her see that you are not going to react with anger, resentment, or bitterness, and that you are calm, centered, and approachable should she decide to reach out in the future.

If she reaches out months after the breakup, she may be interested in reconnecting at some level. This is true even if she reaches out with an indirect approach like, "How's your dog?" or something random. I'll help you navigate this process step-by-step in a later chapter.

How long should this last?
Again, every relationship is different. She may reach out to you very soon after seizing contact. She may not. There's no set-in-stone rule for how long you should cease contact or when you should expect her to reach out. However, this is what I've seen over my coaching career, and you can use it as a general guideline based on the length of the relationship:

- Together for 0-12 months: Expect 1-3 months without contact
- Together for 1-4 years: Expect 3-6 months without contact
- Together for 5-10 years: Expect 6+months without contact

Ultimately, the timeline shouldn't be followed like a set of laws. Besides, however long it takes isn't what's most important; this is a time for you to be focused on *your* life. If you follow the steps outlined in later chapters, you won't be sitting around waiting for some magical amount of time to pass like a kid waiting for the school bell to ring. You'll be out in the real world, building an epic life, meeting new people, and transforming yourself into the man you've always wanted to be. From that work and self-improvement, you can have the opportunity to re-enter a relationship with your ex from a place of power and abundance if you decide to.

But won't she forget about me if I give her too much space?
Your fear is that if you don't *do* something, she'll forget about you and move on. But this isn't how psychology works. If you've been intimate with someone for months, years, or even decades, you aren't as forgettable as you fear. That's especially true when you stop the weak, needy behaviors that drove her away in the first place and project strength by respecting her decision to break up, gracefully bowing out with your dignity intact.

Once she is forced to fully experience the loss of you, she may revisit her decision to end the relationship and possibly reach out. Feelings and love do not vanish when you give someone space and time. Often feelings, emotions and love increase in the absence of someone you care for.

Humans are meant to bond, connect with, and love other people. Love and attachment are two of the most powerful drivers of action and emotion. The best way for her to experience these drivers is for you to take space away from her and spend this time improving your life and spending it with those who want to be in your life, not chasing those who don't.

What if I see her at a social event or gathering?

I want to be clear that ceasing contact doesn't mean you need to jump behind the bushes if you see her. If alcohol is involved at this event and you think you or she may become overly intoxicated, I would avoid going since the risk of something negative happening increases.

Your social circles and lifestyles may overlap. If they do, there's a good chance you'll see her at different events and gatherings. If this happens and you do encounter her, stay grounded and calm. Be brief, respectful, and polite.

Avoid at all costs being bitter, angry, or resentful or expressing any negative emotions when you interact. Instead, simply be positive, share how you're doing if she asks, wish her the best, and enjoy the rest of the event. Do not be seen frowning, looking hopeless, unsocial, hovering around her or worst stalking her every move.

If you do run into her, then don't ignore her. Just keep it short and casual, there's no need to voluntarily share all the intimate details of your life. Unless she's the one pressing for updates and genuinely wants to have a deeper conversation, keep it simple, upbeat, and straightforward. After the brief encounter just carry on and go back to ceasing contact. If you had a good interaction and left on a high note then she will be reminiscing about you in the following days, which works to your advantage.

What if I see her often for work, have kids or a shared pet?

In some situations, there is no way for you to completely cease contact. Your lives are irrevocably enmeshed and there's no way to avoid being in contact on a regular basis. In these situations, you must simply do your best.

If you work together, keep the relationship professional and avoid talking about your personal life or expressing any negative emotions toward her about the breakup. If you have kids or a pet together, be respectful and polite, but avoid long conversations and sharing intimate details of your life unless it comes from her.

Be positive, respectful and polite but brief and, in the absence of completely ceasing contact, do whatever you can to *limit* the depth and emotions in conversations you have. She'll feel that, and in some cases, she can be more affected because she has to physically see you but can't experience intimacy with you in the way she used to. Remember, she ended the relationship, so you are only giving her what she asked for.

What if I cheated?
Apologize in a genuine way and take ownership of your mistake. You'll still need to cease contact and allow a period of space and time to yourselves. Before you do, it's important that she knows how you feel—that you're truly sorry—if there's going to be any chance for her feelings toward you to change while you're not in contact.

"I'm sorry, please forgive me, I love you so much" won't cut it. For your apology to be effective, it must include:

- Acknowledgement of Responsibility: Own up to the fact that what you did was wrong, that it was on *you* and only you, and acknowledge how it made her feel.
- Explanation of What Went Wrong: Dig deep into why you cheated and what you learned from your mistake.
- Expression of Regret: Make it clear that you regret your actions and feel horrible about how this hurt her.
- An Offer to Repair: State the action you're going to take in the future to ensure this never happens again.
- Request for Forgiveness: Ask her to forgive what you did.
- For example:

"I wanted to reach out to let you know how deeply sorry I am for what I did. There are no excuses for my actions, and I can't imagine how it must have felt to have someone you loved betray your trust and loyalty the way that I did. The truth is, I'd been feeling a distance growing between us for a long time and I was scared. I didn't know how to handle what I was feeling and instead of opening up to you about it, I tried to escape from my emotions—and I hurt the person I loved the most in the process.

"If I could turn back the clock and take it back, I would. But I can't. I'm going to do everything I can to be a better man in the future. I don't expect you to take me back and I understand if you never want to speak with me again. But I didn't feel right leaving things the way they were. I hope you can forgive me, and I hope you know that despite what I did, I love you very much."

After this, you cease contact. Stating this once is enough. If you emailed, texted, wrote a letter, or left this as a voice mail, do not follow up to see if she got it. She did. The ball is in her court if she wants to speak with you again or not.

What if I broke up with her?
Similar to cheating, if you left *her,* then it's on you to be clear that you regret your decision and want to try again. However, since you didn't directly break her trust, you can send a text as simple as:

"After having some space and time to reflect, I know that I've made a mistake. I do value you, I do love you, and would like to connect." You can attach a single happy photo of you two together to that text from your phone. Do not send her a dozen photos. Just a good one.

That's it. After you've made your intentions clear, then proceed to cease all contact until she reaches out and asks to reconnect.

It may take weeks or months, so give her space and allow her to process her own emotions. There's nothing more for you to say but chasing or pleading will only reduce your value and make her more likely to agree with your initial decision.

WHAT HAPPENS NOW?

Now that you understand the foundational concepts required to reverse the power dynamic after a breakup, the next question becomes, "What do I do now?"

Ceasing contact is necessary, but it isn't sufficient. If you remove yourself from your ex's life without doing any self-work, you won't grow as a man, understand what went wrong, and learn the lessons from the failed relationship and what could change. Then no lasting change will happen, whether you want her back or want a new partner.

Instead, the goal is to reinvest the newfound time, energy, and mental space created by ceasing contact. This investment is in *yourself.* Your personal growth, your life, your goals, dreams, and passions, all of those things will now get the time and energy you were putting into a relationship. You aren't going to sit on the couch waiting for her to call, drinking booze and scrolling on your phone until midnight. You'll be occupied with reinventing yourself as a man for yourself, which will help you look at your relationship with a clear lens. You'll be equipped to decide for yourself whether or not you want to pursue a future with your ex, and that choice will come from a place of power and abundance rather than scarcity and fear.

In the next chapter, I'm going to show you how to embark on this incredible journey.

BIG IDEAS:

1. **Your Ex Isn't 100% Sure That She Made the Right Decision.**
   No matter how cold or distant she seems now or how many horrible things she's said during the breakup, your ex isn't 100% certain she made the right decision. How you show up post breakup will determine whether she decides it was the right thing to do or was a mistake worth reconsidering.

2. **The Scales of Power Must Be Shifted for Anything Positive to Happen.**
   During the breakup and immediately after it, she is the prize. Any attempt to reconcile or get answers when she holds all the power will backfire. The weak, needy behavior most men exude after a breakup will only increase her power while diminishing your own. To restore balance and regain your power, you must do the opposite of what is expected: make yourself scarce and focus on *yourself* and your growth… not her.

3. **You Must Give Her What She Asked For.**
   Temporarily cease contact with your ex. No visits, no phone calls, no texts, and no social media contact or stalking. Following her every move will destroy your growth, guarantee that if she did reach out you won't be ready, and make the breakup significantly harder to recover from.

   Removing yourself from her life eliminates neediness and humiliation, allowing her to reminisce about positive times you shared. It plants the seeds of desire that can potentially lead to reconnecting. Do not ignore her if she reaches out, yet take your time.

CHAPTER 4:

THE ART OF SHIFTING FROM SCARCITY TO ABUNDANCE

FILLING THE VOID

No matter how deeply you internalized the lessons from the previous chapter or how fervently you believe in the concepts I shared, there's a major obstacle you must overcome on your path to recovery:

Accepting and embracing the journey ahead of you.

Even when you understand what's at stake and you accept that the best possible path is to fully commit to your growth and reinvention as a man, the path isn't easy. It's how you handle the temptation to reach out to her that will determine the outcome of your journey. Which brings us to the next part of this strategy: filling the void left by her absence.

Simply ceasing contact is necessary, but it's not *sufficient*. How are you going to spend this extra time?

If you've ever overcome an addiction or know someone who has, you'll notice something interesting about the recovery process. Very few people ever "break" an addiction, it simply shifts form. This is why sobriety meetings are often filled by people chain smoking cigarettes, chewing tobacco, and pounding cups of coffee.

Removing a vice, addiction, or pattern in and of itself isn't enough. To withstand the emotional onslaught of temptation, you need to develop new outlets and life-giving activities to fill your time and prevent you from reaching out to her, chasing her, begging for her to return. You have to seek out a healthy replacement to increase your value as a man and not fall into a downward spiral of escapism, which will guarantee failure.

A man on this path has one of two options to replace the "high" of contacting and pursuing his ex: vices or growth.

BREAKING THE VICE GRIP

I'd love to tell you that you shouldn't have any vices after your breakup, but my goal in writing this book is to provide men with a realistic roadmap for recovery. Part of that realism is accepting that—regardless of the form it takes—most men will fall prey to some sort of vice, destructive pattern, or habit following a breakup. That's even if *you* broke up with her.

Yes, in an ideal world, you'd be able to immediately shift into a growth-focused life and begin working toward your dreams. If you're the type of man who's capable of making that transition from the start, then absolutely do it. However, the truth is that for most men there will be a period of time where vices are their outlet for coping with the loss of their lover.

Whether it's porn, alcohol, pills, video games, weed, or other substances, it's common. It helps to ease the pain, calm your nerves and anxiety, or sleep better as you adjust to your new reality. There's a reason that surgeons give patients morphine before and after a surgery. Sometimes, the pain of an experience is too great to bear on our own, yet it should not become habitual.

So rather than standing on a soapbox and telling you to avoid all vices—advice that even I've struggled to follow post-breakup—my invitation is to engage in your vices with complete awareness of what you're doing. Rather than haphazardly abusing substances or distractions to ease your situation, understand exactly how you'll engage with your vices, how long you'll engage with them, and what type of support you'll need to ensure that you don't become lost in them indefinitely and make the situation worse.

I want to be clear. This isn't a hall pass to drink, use drugs, have meaningless sex, or sedate to your heart's content. And I'm in no way encouraging you to engage in destructive behaviors at all. I'd recommend you stay away from them. Rather, I'm acknowledging that a brief period of sedation and distraction may happen, regardless of what I say.

The bottom line is, if you have the willpower and resolve to avoid vices altogether, do it. If you don't? Then own your power and create clear terms and support systems around your vices, like asking a friend, family member, mentor, or coach to check in and hold you accountable.

As a final note, I want to make it clear that there is one vice you must avoid at all costs, one that will be more tempting than liquor, drugs, or porn ever could: daydreaming about your ex for too long and too often.

If you remove yourself from your ex's life only to spend your days obsessing over her, crying over old photos, ogling nude photos of her, and thinking about all of the good times you shared together or stalking her on social media, then the scales of power will remain in her favor indefinitely regardless of how much space you allow. Whether she bears witness to this or not, if the time comes to reconnect, your lack of growth and obsessive focus on *her* will be obvious and downright unattractive.

Living in the past and reminiscing about your ex is nothing more than a form of self-inflicted emotional suicide. You are voluntarily injecting emotional pain into your life with each look like a heroin addict. I get it, it feels good to do this, yet it doesn't advance your life in any way and slows down your recovery if you want to get over her. So what is most important right now? You need to do everything in your power to live in the here and now. Whatever is happening in front of you with your own two eyes is your actual reality. Make each moment, each day, each month count. Shift your focus to yourself, your own growth, and your own evolution. It's the only path to reclaiming your power as a man and having the opportunity to get her back or eventually find a new partner.

THE CORE COMMITMENTS TO BECOME YOUR STRONGEST SELF

To transform yourself into the type of man who's capable of re-attracting his ex or attracting a higher-quality woman, and to ensure that you don't fall into the same self-defeating cycle in the future, you must accept something important:

No one is coming to save you.

Not your ex, not your friends, not your family. The responsibility for growth and moving forward is on you alone. Of all the variables playing into the breakup equation, the single most important one is YOU. It's your willingness to take action, to embrace discomfort, and to drive forward when your brain is screaming "I'm in pain" or "I want to reach out to her."

I'm not saying this to discourage you, but rather to prepare you for what's to come. Initially, the path will seem painful and unrelenting. You won't *want* to take the action required of you. You'll want to run, hide, and escape, to say "screw this." You'll want to reach out to her to calm your anxiety, crawl back to her or fall into excessive distractions and likely make the situation worse.

But the key question you must ask yourself is this: "What story do I want to write for myself?"

Right now, you have a choice between defeat and victory, between allowing this experience to break you and answering the call to adventure. You can become the high-value man that you know you're capable of, a man who uses this newfound time and space as a catalyst for personal transformation, or you can fall and prove your ex right.

Will you ascend to new levels of being because of this experience? Or will you be beaten by it and fall into darkness for years to come? That choice is yours. Whatever action you choose, you'll begin to build momentum in your life. But what direction will that momentum carry you in?

If you commit to the path ahead of you fully, you'll experience a healthy season of positive momentum. The rising tide of action will ascend all aspects of your life. Your life will expand, creativity will emerge and you'll feel a sense of personal power and confidence you likely haven't experienced in years.

But if you choose *not* to commit, you will enter a downward spiral of personal destruction. It leads to stagnation, lowered value, weak behavior, and repeating the mistakes of the past over and over again, either with your ex or new women.

The more action towards growth you take, the more motivated you become to continue that forward momentum—and the more terrifying it becomes to fall back into disempowering patterns and behaviors.

The path ahead of you isn't easy and you will suffer emotionally and physically at times. But it *is* necessary, and it's a part of the process laid out before you. If you're willing, this experience can serve as the impetus for a whole new way of life. Regardless of the outcome, you'll look back on this event years from now and feel grateful for the man you've become.

To make this a reality, there are core commitments you must make:

I. Transform Your Physical and Mental Health
II. Achieve Higher Levels of Professional Success
III. Revive Lost Passions
IV. Build a Quality Social Circle and Meet New Women
V. Create an Unwavering Emotional Support System

I want to be clear, the path to these commitments is not well-paved and easy to walk. Progress will not happen in a linear fashion. It will be messy, confusing, and painful at times. You'll feel like you're doing well and moving on just fine, only to experience a trigger that sends you into an emotional storm and feel like you're starting over from zero. You may have a days or weeks where you adhere to each of the commitments flawlessly only to fall right back into your old vices, distractions and temptations to obsess over your ex's every move. Although I encourage you to aim for the ideal of following each of these commitments every day, the true measurement of success is progress.

Every day and week, your aim is to be just a little bit stronger, more resilient, and more powerful than you were the before, even if it's just by one percent. If you fall off the wagon and fail to make progress on these core commitments, give yourself grace and accept it as a part of any worthwhile journey. Don't make excuses or alibis for procrastination but remember that you're going through a traumatic and difficult transition in life. It's okay that you aren't perfect every day, but it's essential that you're making progress overtime. Measure success on a monthly basis. If you stay consistent, then every 4-8 weeks you will transform into an upgraded version of yourself, feeling stronger, happier and more optimistic about the present and future.

So, when you face setbacks—and you will—simply pick yourself up and keep pressing forward best you can. With enough time and focus, you'll come out the other side a whole new man with a big fat smile on your face.

Now that the expectations are clear, let's dive into the commitments.

I. TRANSFORM YOUR PHYSICAL AND MENTAL HEALTH

During the breakup, your physiology was quite literally under attack. The supply of hormones and neurochemicals that create motivation, contentment, and pleasure fell to an all-time low. In fact, according to research conducted by sociologist Dr. Linda J. Waite of the University of Chicago, individuals who are widowed or divorced are 20% more likely to develop chronic health conditions ranging from cancer to heart disease to diabetes.

Even though there are plenty of ways to mitigate the damage—and individuals in the study who remarried saw a dramatic reduction in these conditions—the fact remains that breakups and divorces are intensely stressful experiences that can wreak havoc on your health *if* you let them. That makes it more important than ever for you to fully commit to the journey of health and physical growth. You're already in a low state psychologically, emotionally, and physically. In fact, you may have been neglecting your health long before the breakup... and almost certainly after it.

My goal with this section isn't to turn you into a superhuman athlete, but rather to create a scenario where you're doing everything in your power to ensure proper mental and physical health. That allows you to show up to the rest of the commitments with greater drive and effectiveness and to protect against the inevitable emotional storms of the post-breakup experience. Without your health, you are fighting a muddy uphill battle.

Now, this isn't a diet or workout book. I'm not a doctor and this is *not* medical advice. There are plenty of experts who can provide more breakdowns of the protocols you can follow to lose fat, gain muscle, and boost your energy and mood.

But I *do* want to share some core principles and practices that have served me and my clients well.

1. Train Hard. Move Daily.

Everyone reading this will have a different level of health and fitness that lends itself to different programs or routines. But as a general recommendation, I encourage you to train (e.g., lifting heavy weights or doing cardio) at least three times a week and to get outside for at least 20 minutes a day. This could be walking, jogging, cycling, hiking, or any kind of sport—anything active that gets you in the sun.

With regular exercise you'll be amazed at how quickly your mental and emotional state will improve. Just like stagnant water breeds bacteria and disease, so too does a stagnant mind and body breed depression, anxiety, and loneliness. The goal is to create a state in which negative thoughts and emotions cannot thrive, and instead positive thoughts and emotions can. The best way to start working toward this goal is through consistent and challenging movement.

Remember, *motion* creates *emotion*. When you change your physical state, you change your emotional state. Even if everything else in your life feels like it's going downhill, you have the power to make time for yourself each day to move, sweat, and exercise your body and mind.

When you challenge yourself physically and boost your mood, everything else flows.

The pain of the breakup will start to diminish because you're exercising your body regularly and getting the endorphins and dopamine you need to regulate your mental and emotional states. By challenging yourself with strenuous physical activity, you'll develop a greater level of confidence in your ability to overcome the psychological pressure of staying committed to the reversal of power and focusing inward on personal growth. The lack of motion will create an uphill battle that will make this journey all but impossible.

Your self-esteem and confidence have taken a blow from the rejection, and the fastest way to reclaim them is by pushing yourself physically. When you feel heartbroken and alone, keep moving. When you feel beaten down and burned out, keep moving. When you want to stare at old photos or reach out to her with another desperate plea, keep going. When you want to cave into vices and distractions to distract from the pain, keep moving.

If you stay in motion consistently, the momentum will build, and positive results will follow.

2. Eat Real Foods

To win the mental battle, you need clean energy. Without it, you'll fail to stay in motion and succumb to vices and unhealthy distractions.

One of the many unique challenges of a breakup is you'll be thrust into a naturally low-energy state. You likely won't have much of an appetite during or immediately after. You won't have the energy to grocery shop, cook and clean. When the cravings hit, you'll be tempted to fall into a daily habit of fast food and frozen food with tons of sodium, preservatives and sugar.

These habits will end up diminishing your energy and mood even further, causing brain fog, weight gain, and lowered levels of confidence. If you're in this state, it's unlikely that you can do the work in this book, re attract your ex or any new partner.

In anticipation of this, I recommend using meal replacement shakes and healthy pre-made meals from the grocery store or delivery services if you can. My personal go-to is a strawberry, blueberry, banana smoothie with a handful of spinach, kale, a few scoops of protein powder, and a serving of maca green tea with almond milk, but this is a great time to experiment in the kitchen, develop new cooking routines and find what works for you.

My diet recommendation is simple: eat real foods.

That's it. If something grew in the ground or had a heartbeat—and your body feels good when you consume it—then eat it. If it's wrapped in cellophane and processed with a slew of chemicals you can't pronounce, skip it.

If you want to accelerate your health journey, you can layer in intermittent fasting—eating all of your calories within a set eight-hour window every day—to improve your mood, cognition, and body composition even faster. Do your research on this before trying, but it has been beneficial for me in weight loss and provides an increase in energy and focus during the day. I eat only between the hours of 10am and 6pm.

After my last breakup, I lost more than 25 pounds in about ten weeks by following these steps. I trained hard several times a week, ate real food, and fasted. I felt and looked amazing, which boosted my confidence and levels of energy at a time when they were at their lowest post breakup.

3.   Sleep Like a Baby with No Guilt

The most often overlooked principle of health is to prioritize deep rest. If you aren't fully resting and recovering, you won't have the willpower to follow through on the other commitments in this chapter. You'll be more susceptible to doing things that devalue you through weak behaviors or engage in unhealthy vices.

When you're chronically sleep deprived, your prefrontal cortex (the executive center of your brain responsible for willpower and decision making) becomes severely weakened. In many studies, sleep deprived drivers performed worse than individuals who were drunk. When you consider the number of bad decisions men make when they're under the influence of alcohol, consider how chronic sleep deprivation could compromise your ability to think rationally and act in a powerful way.

On the most fundamental level, this means that getting seven to eight hours of quality sleep every night. It's one of the most important actions you can take following a breakup.

To ensure this happens, I encourage you to:

- Go to bed and wake up at the same time every day.
- Take a short ten to fifteen-minute walk in the early morning sunlight to regulate your circadian rhythm.
- Invest in blackout shades, a great mattress, and sleep aids like magnesium and l-theanine. Look into calming teas like chamomile or passionflower before bedtime.
- Avoid technology and bright lights at least two hours before bed (the blue light disrupts your sleep cycles).

However, you must be careful not to use sleep to hide from your reality. Sleeping fewer than five hours a night doesn't serve your growth, but neither will sleeping more than ten hours and avoiding the real world under the covers. Get the rest you need to feel recovered and energized, then go crush the day!

But beyond sleep, it's important to prioritize real rest during the weeks and months immediately following your breakup. For most people, their definition of rest is binge watching television while knocking back a few beers. But according to research in the *Journal of Media Psychology*, it's an incredibly inefficient way to recover from a stressful time.

Television and video games create a flurry of activity in your visual cortex—the center of your brain responsible for processing images—and as a result, they prevent you from shifting out of focused and engaged "beta brain waves" into a relaxed "alpha state."

On the other hand, activities like talking with a friend, meditating, reading, playing an instrument, going for a walk, hiking, or cooking a meal allow your brain to slow down and remain calm. That can result in deeper relaxation, and more mental bandwidth to fully process the heightened emotions you're dealing with.

Digital distractions should be reduced or eliminated, at least for a while. But one major benefit of a "digital diet" is you'll carry these healthy habits with you moving forward. For the long term, you'll reap the benefits as this lifestyle change brings you more energy, clarity, focus, and drive. This is a major win for your future as you reclaim so much wasted time.

4. Treat Yourself Leveraging the "Halo Effect" for Increased Confidence
Finally, I encourage you to leverage the "halo effect"—the theory that improving your appearance improves every other area of your life. Invest in updating your wardrobe with new clothes that fit better and make you feel more confident (you'll be saving a lot of money post-breakup, and this is a worthwhile investment to improve your self-esteem). Get a haircut and upgrade your grooming equipment and products. Get some facial cleansers, moisturizers, teeth whitening, and anti-aging serums. Changing your physical appearance can symbolically cement your commitment to transformation during this process and remain a part of your identity moving forward.

It may seem superficial, but the way you present yourself on the outside has a profound impact on the way you feel about yourself and the way others perceive you. If you fail to invest in your physical appearance, you're stacking the deck against you. Why? We want every advantage we can get during this time of recovery.

II. ACHIEVE HIGHER LEVELS OF PROFESSIONAL SUCCESS

Immediately following a breakup, you've experienced a major blow to your sense of worth and ego, a blow that many men let dampen their spirits as they go about their daily lives, prolonging the recovery process. However, hidden in this pain is also the gift of focus, energy, and drive, if channeled productively.

You have extra time on your hands with this person out of your life. You no longer have to consider her schedule and her needs. This gives you the opportunity to channel the pain you're experiencing into the positive drivers of your professional life.

The pain of the breakup makes the challenges and struggles of your professional life seem minor in comparison. When weighed against the pain of losing someone you loved, the pain of working extra hours, pushing through a demanding project, or taking a new risk suddenly weigh far less.

I invite you to use this extra time to your advantage. You have an opportunity to raise your standards, pursue big goals, and demand *more* for your future than you ever did in the past. Doing great work and getting paid more for your effort creates a powerful ripple effect. You'll feel more confident, have more opportunities, and experience an increase in your self-worth. By fully committing to this journey, you'll magnetically attract higher-quality people—including new women.

Like attracts like. High-quality people are attracted to other individuals who are positive, thriving, and progressing in life, while being repelled by those who are stagnating, depressed, and stuck in a victim mentality of blaming others. If you find yourself regularly caught in toxic relationships or struggling to attract the right types of people in your life, I challenge you to consider how you are showing up to life. Are you the type of person you want to attract? Are you showing up as the type of man that your dream woman would love to be with?

While it is not a complete solution, a commitment to professional excellence is an effective way to increase your confidence and self-worth. It will attract more opportunities, higher-quality relationships, and more freedom.

This doesn't mean work 80+ hours a week or drown yourself in work to escape from the emotions of the breakup. But rather, it's an invitation to achieve higher levels of excellence in your career. It doesn't have to take more hours to be more successful, either, it just requires making the hours you already have more effective, productive, and results driven. Work smarter and more efficiently, not harder and longer is my motto.

Here are a few principles that will create a much-needed cascade of growth and momentum in your professional life.

1. Commit to Excellence

Many men half-ass their way through life. They do the bare minimum to get by, not just in their careers, but in their relationships, their bodies, and their social lives. Chances are your breakup was caused at least in part by this kind of pattern of "half-assery," which is exactly what makes the commitment to excellence so important moving forward.

When you commit to doing your work to your fullest potential, whether you love it or not, you'll begin shifting your identity as a man. You're no longer going to be someone who does great work only when he feels like it, or really performs only when he's motivated, and things are going well in life. You're the type of man who commits *fully*, regardless of how you're feeling that day.

This is not to be mistaken for sacrificing your soul at the altar of material success. Rather, it is an invitation to become more intentional, focused, and results-oriented in the hours you have. Even if you can't see it yet, this season of training will empower you to embrace new opportunities when they arise and condition you to show up fully to every commitment in your life and put an end to a life of "half-assery."

Here are a handful of practices that will make this easier.

- **Plan Every Day the Night Before** and commit to doing everything you plan. This will force you to ruthlessly eliminate ineffective, unnecessary tasks and train you to develop integrity with your goals. You're going to do what you say you're going to do.
- **Embrace the Power of "One More"** and when you think you're done, go just a little bit further. Make that extra call. Finish one more task. Condition yourself to do just a little bit more than is required and you will become the type of person who goes above and beyond.
- **Leverage Cyclical Recovery** by working on a timer and commit to ninety minutes of fully-focused work followed by ten to fifteen minutes of intentional rest and recovery. Even in your relationships, time apart is just as important as time together.
- **Eliminate the Distractions and Temptations** so instead of stealing from your future by wasting time on mindless distractions like social media or watching addictive videos, you stay focused and fully present with whatever you're doing. Turn off your wifi,

put your phone in another room, install a website blocker. Do whatever you need to do to show up fully to your goals everyday.

2. Embrace the Magic of Thinking Big

Excellence isn't simply about doing more work, it's about daring to dream bigger, to raising your standards and tolerating only the best for yourself. During this season, spend time revisiting your goals and dreams. What are the *big* goals you've always wanted to achieve but put on pause because you were bogged down by the relationship?

Do you want to get a promotion at work? Start your own business? Write a book? Start a podcast or YouTube channel? If you knew that you could create any reality you wanted for yourself, what would that reality look like (personally, professionally, romantically)? I encourage you to really contemplate this question deeply for an entire weekend, maybe while going on a hike in nature, as it has the power to transform your life beyond anything that happens with your ex.

When you step out of the status quo and decide to pursue the big soul-igniting goals that most men take with them to the grave, it creates a feeling of aliveness, excitement, and vibrancy that you absolutely need right now. Like a doctor using a defibrillator to restart a patient's heart, envisioning exciting goals will jumpstart your soul and jolt you out of your current weakened state.

Over the next ninety days, I encourage you to pick one or two big goals you've always wanted to achieve and begin working toward them every single day.

> **You must become a man on a mission, not a lost, hopeless, heartbroken man aimlessly wandering through life obsessing over his ex.**

The drive and focus required to achieve bigger goals, whether they're professional or not, will keep you from caving and reaching out to your ex. Even better, they will inject more purpose into your life that goes beyond your breakup.

When you're busy creating an exciting life, you won't have the time, energy, or desire to fawn after your ex. You'll be moving in a new direction that awakens your spirit and drives your life forward. If she wants to join, she'll have to chase you and jump on board and follow your lead, because you're building a grander life with or without her.

Consider how much more attractive this frame is to her and any other women you wish to attract, as well as how much more empowering it is for you. Human beings want to win. They want to feel like they're getting the best option possible. If you're chasing, pursuing, and making her your sole aim in life, that means she's the prize and you're clearly not. But when you're building something in your life and pursuing big goals regardless of her actions, it shows that *you* have priorities and you're busy going after them. You aren't doing this for her respect or approval. It's about the feeling of aliveness that progressing towards big goals gives you.

3. Invest in Your Skills

If you aren't where you want to be in your career right now, there's a simple reason. Your skills probably haven't been sufficiently developed to deserve the level of success and respect you want.

Barring trust fund babies and lottery winners, the most successful men all became that way by developing valuable skills. Whether it was leadership, sales, marketing, coding, recruiting, systems, speaking, writing, or negotiation, their financial and professional success can always be attributed in part to a set of skills that allowed them to provide more value to the marketplace than average men.

But beyond the financial impact, the act of developing new skills has profound implications on your relationships and recovery post-breakup. By going through the process of skill acquisition, like embracing the fact that you're mediocre at something you should be better at and putting in the work to improve, you'll begin to develop a stronger growth mindset.

When you realize that everything in life is about mindset and skills and that everything can be improved upon over time, the challenges in other areas of your life won't seem as daunting. If you can point to specific times where you overcame your own ignorance and ineptitude by developing a new professional skill, it will give you greater confidence as you develop other skills, like talking to women, dating, or relationships. The act of professional development will prove to you through *action and results* that everything is "figure-outable" and that, with enough time, effort, and optimization, any goal is possible.

If you never develop high-value skills, you will always struggle professionally and be competing for average pay. To put this into practice, I want you to ask yourself:

"What is the *one* skill that, if mastered, would allow me to significantly increase my professional and financial success in the near- and long-term future?"

Then, once you have your answer, devote time each day to developing that skill with this newfound freedom you have. I recommend keeping a record of your progress so that you can look back and see how far you've come, which helps you stay on the path when it seems like no progress is being made.

4. Embrace the "Mastermind Effect"

Author Dan Sullivan is famous for a simple but profound idea: Whenever you're feeling stuck in your life or business, ask yourself, "Who, not how." That means, instead of asking, "How do I solve this problem myself?" consider instead, "Who has already solved this problem and can help me?"

Every big leap I've ever taken was the result of being exposed to new ideas or strategies from someone who had already achieved what I wanted to achieve or by using the support of allies (which we'll talk about in a moment) to ensure I did what I needed to do.

No man is an island. And no matter how smart or successful you are, we all need support to get to the next level—otherwise, we'd be there already. So, instead of trying to figure everything out on your own, I encourage you to enlist the help of mentors, coaches, and guides who have already "been there, done that."

This is true in your health and fitness, and it's why hiring a personal trainer or nutritionist is a good idea. It's also true in your relationships and in your career.

To put this concept into practice, write down a list of *every* problem you're currently facing in your professional life. It could be a skill you're struggling to develop, a problem at work you don't know how to solve, or feeling like you don't know how to pivot to a new career or start your own business to escape from a job you hate.

Now ask yourself, "Who do I know who has already solved this problem, and how can I get them to help me?"

Do you need to hire a coach or mentor and pay to get access to the tools and resources you need? If you don't know anyone personally, is there an expert who's already written a book or created a course to help you solve this problem? Do you need to simply text someone in your network and ask them out for a coffee?

Figure out who can help you and then *ask*.

Do you want my help? Learn more about the work I do with men: knowledgeformen.com/grow

III. REVIVE LOST PASSIONS

A passionate man is an attractive man. Regardless of what the passion is, most women are drawn to men who are all-in on unique hobbies and pursuits. And whether it's music, art, photography, surfing, martial arts, or outdoor adventures, one of the most valuable things you can do following a breakup is to rekindle lost passions and develop new ones that excite you.

Whether it's creating art, backpacking through the wilderness to capture the perfect photo, or playing epic twelve-bar blues with new friends, new passions and hobbies create new opportunities for adventures, social connections, and ultimately, lead to a more interesting and vibrant life. These pursuits are doubly important if your career isn't a great source of pride and purpose because they give you a positive outlet to keep you busy in the absence of your ex, while simultaneously increasing your value and attractiveness.

Again, this doesn't mean that you need to quit your job and start busking on street corners to become a more attractive man, simply that intentionally cultivating new interests, hobbies, and passions is beneficial for your recovery.

Here are a few of the most effective ways to make this happen:

1. Cultivate a T-Shaped Life

The most effective framework I've found for accomplishing this is something called the "T-Shaped Life." When you look at the most interesting, attractive men, they all share a common pattern. They had a depth of mastery in one core domain—typically their career—and a vast swath of competency in other interests and skills.

Ernest Hemingway was a master author and commander of the written word, but he was also a competent outdoorsman, linguist, boxer, marksman, soldier, and socialite. Teddy Roosevelt was a world class politician and leader, but also a skilled hunter, writer, naturalist, explorer, and boxer. Winston Churchill was arguably one of the most prominent political figures in the last few generations, and also a painter, bricklayer, and card hustler.

The good news is becoming a "T-Shaped" man is easier today than it's ever been. With a plethora of online learning platforms and courses, you can develop a basic level of competency in almost any skill imaginable. Write down a list of every skill, topic, or hobby that interests you. Pick the top three that have the lowest barrier to entry (meaning, they don't require huge sums of money or travel to develop) and schedule time each week to begin practicing them.

Every minute you spend developing a new skill or educating yourself on a new topic is a minute that you're focused on *yourself* and your growth as a man, *not* on your ex and what she is doing or unhealthy vices. The more you can fill your days with exciting new pursuits, the less likely you are to be tempted to reach out to your ex or live a life of distraction. If you *do* reconnect with her, you'll have new interests and hobbies that increase your attractiveness and give you plenty to talk about.

2. Indulge in "Passionate Distractions"

In an ideal world, you would spend 90% of your time focused on your growth, career, health, passions, and social life, and less than 10% of your time on distractions like TV, video games, or scrolling social media.

But the modern world is designed to keep us distracted. Instead of fighting this, learn to transmute your distractions into a way to develop your passions.

For example, instead of binging mindless programs, watch documentaries, educational podcasts, and online courses. If you are going to use social media, then go through your social media accounts and unfollow negative or wasteful ones. Instead, fill your feed with content related to your interests and passions so you can pick up new ideas and concepts while you scroll, yet keep this to a minimum as this can be a form of distraction as well.

It's a small shift, but over time, you'll expand your horizons and become far more interesting than the average guy who spends all of his downtime gaming or watching a re-run of his favorite show.

3. Lean into Social Passions

Commit to at least *one* passion that gives you the opportunity to expand your social life.

In the next section, we'll dive into the details of how (and why) to develop a stronger social network and attract new women. One of the simplest ways to start is by picking up a new skill or hobby that makes you get out of your home and into the real world.

Things like martial arts, CrossFit, yoga, dancing, recreational sport leagues, and other groups or clubs can prove invaluable to your recovery. You'll establish new friendships, meet new women, and create new sources of connection to ease the inevitable isolation and loneliness post breakup.

IV. IMPROVE YOUR SOCIAL LIFE AND MEET NEW WOMEN

In a Harvard study of adult development, multiple researchers followed the lives of 724 men in an attempt to answer a simple question: "What makes for a life well-lived?" Participants ranged from U.S. presidents to multi-millionaires to alcoholics to schizophrenics... and the results were eye opening.

The single most important factor in the quality of one's life is the quality of their relationships. Money, social status, and material success increased their subjective wellbeing and happiness to some degree. But it was relationships that trumped every factor.

The great irony is that, despite its importance, most men approach their social life in a haphazard, unintentional way. They might have a clear plan for their career, their finances, and their fitness, yet when it comes to the single most important area of their lives? They settle for the occasional beer with a buddy from high school, college, work or neighbor that they hardly resonate with.

Nothing will have a more profound impact on your ability to recover from a breakup than your social support system.

Human beings are hardwired to be social creatures. We need connection and community to thrive, which is exactly why breakups are so devastating. Following a breakup, you lose your primary source of connection. But thanks to your hunter-gatherer programming, your brain believes you have not only lost all connection in the present, you may have lost your future opportunities for connection as well. Your brain is freaking out, causing panic, anxiety, and despair.

We spent most of our history as a species living in small tribes of around 100 people. A "breakup" could be a literal death sentence. Intense feelings of scarcity were not only accurate, but necessary to ensure survival. A breakup signals to the brain that you lost your best chance at procreating and ensuring the survival of your genes. Your value in the tribe decreased, and your opportunities to find a new partner were small, if not nonexistent.

Thankfully, we aren't living in an era where this is true anymore. Within a thirty-mile radius, there are likely dozens, if not hundreds of quality women you could build a life with and experience a connection that is equal or greater than the connection you shared with your ex. But your brain doesn't see it this way, and the only way to escape from the evolutionary scarcity and step into the abundance available to you is to experience it firsthand.

You have to prove to yourself through action and daily exposure that you haven't lost your only source of connection and that there are many attractive women around you that would want to meet and connect with you. Without having an abundance of social experiences, you're more likely to spend your time post-breakup wallowing in isolation and succumbing to unhealthy behaviors that feel good in the short term, but make the situation worse in the long term. But when your social calendar is packed each week, you're less likely to sabotage the progress you're making.

This isn't about escaping from the pain by drowning yourself in a sea of meaningless sex or partying. Rather, you need to become more attractive by creating an "anti-fragile" social circle where you're regularly meeting new people—both men and women—elevating your personal status, and creating a flywheel of abundance, adventure, and invigorating experiences that make you come alive.

The good news is, creating an epic social circle filled with like-minded men and beautiful women (even if you don't pursue a sexual relationship with them) is fairly simple. It requires a bit of leadership, creativity, and effort. But when compared to the alternative of sitting at home alone and binge-watching adult sites while stalking your ex's social media, the demands are far outweighed by the benefits.

More importantly, the time and focus required to build a stronger social circle and the validation, support, and connection it provides will serve to keep your recovery journey on track. When your calendar is booked with fun adventures, dinners with people you enjoy, and epic experiences, you'll be less likely to cave to the temptation to reach out to your ex or waste time living in the past. And whether you want her back or not, when she sees you surrounded by quality people, living a more interesting and vibrant life, and having experiences that *any* woman would want to share in, she'll view you as a more attractive man likely wondering if she made the right decision.

THE SYSTEM TO BUILDING A QUALITY SOCIAL LIFE

1. Rapid Reconnection

Whenever you embark on a new journey, the most important thing you can do is to build fast momentum by identifying and executing "quick wins." This is true in business. It's true in your health. And it's true in your social life.

So, before you begin expanding your social circle and meeting new people, the first step is to simply reconnect with existing friends, family members, and co-workers with whom you've lost touch. Whether it's a sibling, cousin, work associate, college buddy, or childhood friend, we all have people in our lives, especially when we get caught up in a romantic relationship, that we fell out of contact with because life got in the way. So, reach out and reconnect.

Pull out your phone, scroll through your contacts and find five people you haven't connected with in the last six to twelve months and send them a quick text just to check in and see how they're doing, letting them know that you'd love to catch up soon.

"Hey, just thought of you. How are you doing?"

Although you can share that you're going through a breakup once you talk over the phone or meet up in person, I encourage you to stay positive and avoid talking too deeply about these struggles too soon. You aren't trying to use these people as a crutch to get over your ex, and if you're too negative early into the reconnection, your neediness might drive them away. You're simply re-engaging with people who matter to you and re-establishing the connection. Organically, they will likely ask, "How is so and so doing?" which is an opportunity to then briefly share what happened with your ex.

2. Organize Experiences to Foster Community and Connection

Once you've begun reconnecting with the people who are already in your life, the next step is to begin expanding your social circle by organizing meetups and becoming more of a leader in your network. This doesn't mean you need to invest thousands of dollars into crazy house parties or spend weeks planning events and gatherings. Simply work on becoming a source of positive experiences and good times.

An easy way to do this is to host or organize a weekly, low to no-cost event or dinner. Sending a text to a group of people like: "Hey, it's been a while, been wanting to connect, hosting X this week, already have xyz and xyz coming, join us?"

Football Sundays, Taco Tuesdays, Saturday bbq at the park or beach days, or Thursday comedy club nights are all examples of casual, low-key outings you can organize. Have people bring something and it makes it easier for you.

For these events, your goal is to establish a consistent cadence of connection over time, meaning that you organize an event weekly or every other week and encourage your friends to invite other people who might be a good fit. Then, every new person who shows up to the event can be invited back and asked to bring another one of *their* friends.

This can compound quickly and result in weekly gatherings with many people. You don't have to do that, and the goal isn't necessarily to grow these events until you have a huge group renting out a venue on a weekly basis or maybe it is. Rather, you want to expand your social circle enough that you begin connecting with new people. It's your social life, so design it to your liking. What matters is that you do have one, and that it works for you.

Some of the people you meet won't be a good fit for your life. Some of them will be fair weather friends you only see from time to time. But a small handful will slowly enter your core tribe, the people you develop close relationships with and who become an integral part of your life.

Why follow this strategy instead of going out and introducing yourself to strangers? You immediately position yourself as a leader in the social group. You were the one who curated the experience and made sure it actually happened, which elevates your value and increases your status. This makes you more attractive to any person who joins the events and puts you in a position of leadership from a social standpoint.

Just as importantly, this strategy is the most effective way to build the social circle *you* want moving forward. If you start with a handful of friends or acquaintances you already know and like and then ask them to bring likeminded friends, you have an easy way to get introduced to new people who likely share your values and interests. If you try to meet strangers solo at the bar, a gym, or random party, you could waste unnecessary time and get rejected by individuals who aren't even aligned with your personality or lifestyle, and more rejection is the last thing we need right now.

This strategy works, but it can take time to be effective. I have a close friend who followed this blueprint by starting a weekly yoga class on the beach. The class was completely free and began just as a fun way for him to practice yoga with friends. During the early days, it was just him and a few other men doing their downward dogs and looking a little silly. But after a few weeks, more people started to join. By showing up consistently as a leader, he was able to create what became a locally famous event where more than 200 people—most of whom were attractive women—come out every week to participate in his class. Since doing this, he's had a steady stream of dates with quality women without spending money at random bars with random people, and has established himself as a leader in a likeminded community that suits him.

You certainly do not need to create anything of this magnitude, it's just an example of starting small and taking it to whatever size you'd like.

A word of warning: although the core strategy to improve your social life is elegantly simple, it's important that you enter into this journey from a clear, grounded frame. If you aren't careful, it's easy to turn every dinner or get together with friends into a full-blown therapy session where you bring the whole group down by pining over your ex and her latest actions. And even though it's important to build a support network, that isn't the goal of this specific group of people.

The people you're meeting need to "ascend" to your closer circle of friends before they learn more about your inner struggles. Otherwise, the relationships will feel transactional; it will seem like you're only getting people together so you have people to talk to about your ex. If they're mutual friends with you and your ex, you want to avoid these conversations (because the last thing you want is for them to go and tell your ex how heartbroken and hurt you are). I recommend you avoid inviting anyone to these events whose social circle overlaps with your ex's altogether.

The goal of these interactions is to have fun, establish connections, and share positive emotions. That's it. Your family and close friends can help you navigate the deep emotional challenges of your breakup. But the new individuals entering your life don't want to be burdened with your personal struggles so soon, at least not until you've developed a more meaningful friendship.

3.   The Role of New Women Post-Breakup

Navigating connections and relationships with new women immediately following a breakup can be challenging. On one hand, your brain needs to know that you didn't lose the only woman in the world who will love you, and that there are plenty of other women who are interested in you.

On the other hand, you need time and space to fully heal, process, and integrate the lessons from your past relationship. Just as importantly, until you've fully moved on from your breakup, you're going to be in a fragile, low-energy emotional state. If you get rejected by a new woman, the pain of that experience can easily derail your recovery *just* as fast as reaching out to your ex can. Bear in mind that if rejections do happen, it's not entirely your fault; they are not seeing the fully alive and healthy version of you, but instead are experiencing a hurt man who lost someone he loves who is trying his best socially.

So even though it's healthy and even necessary to interact, talk, and socialize with new women, your focus shouldn't be on sleeping with anyone new.

When you go out to socialize, focus on having fun, adding value, and sharing positive experiences without pursuing or initiating any type of sexual interaction. Push the goal of sex or a new relationship completely out of your mind and lead with value, connection, and friendship. Go out with the intention of meeting new people and creating connections with men and women who enjoy your company. The benefit of this is it frees you to be yourself and not worry about any outcome like sex, so you are more likely to enjoy yourself.

By doing this, the energy you bring to social interactions will feel more authentic and genuine than what most women normally experience. As a result, their responses will be much more positive because they can feel that you aren't trying to take anything from them. You aren't trying to impress them. You aren't trying to sleep with them. You're just trying to have fun and share good energy, which is always welcomed.

If romance begins to develop organically as a result of the way you're showing up, then take it slow and don't rush into anything. Be honest and upfront with where you are at on this journey.

4. Strategically Leveraging Social Media

Following a breakup, there are two important roles that social media plays in your recovery and growth. The first is to create new opportunities socially. The second is for those who want their ex back to provide "artifacts of growth" that can indirectly show your ex that you're doing fine without her.

To leverage social media as effectively as possible there are a few general rules to follow:

- Post only one to three times a week (social media should be a tool, not another distraction). Posting too much is trying too hard, which removes the mystery of your whereabouts.
- Post fun content in groups of people, events, adventures, and social activities.
- In the first 90 days, if you post content with women, ensure it's in a group setting with other men and women, not just you and her as this can backfire, coming across as if you are trying to send a message to your ex.
- Remain calm and avoid bragging or talking about the breakup or your ex in posts, saying how you are over her, life is better single, life is so amazing without your ex, etc.

Although it isn't necessary or an essential part of this program, using social media with discipline can accelerate your social results and show your ex that you are thriving in life without her, which can increase your value in her eyes if that is your goal.

V. BUILD AN UNWAVERING EMOTIONAL SUPPORT SYSTEM

Following my last breakup, other areas of my life were on *fire*. I was in the gym several days a week, surfing with friends, running a successful coaching business, podcasting, writing books, and connecting with amazing women and high-caliber men on a weekly basis. Yet despite the abundance and fun in my life, it still hurt to lose my ex. Every time I thought of her, I would have a rush of emotion and was still saddened by the loss of her.

But I was able to withstand temptation and remain grounded in my own power because I had an unwavering emotional support system I could turn to when things got hard. This is the final piece of the equation most men ignore.

You need *trusted* sources of support you can rely on during sudden moments of weakness, heavy emotions, and internal struggle. These are people you trust completely, can be extremely vulnerable with, and with whom you can share every detail of your inner world, knowing that they won't share anything with anyone. Whether they're close friends, parents, siblings, or a coach, every man needs a reliable support structure to help them stand strong in their commitments and do the work required to grow from this experience.

You should communicate and be upfront with these people and share with them what you need over the next few months. The people you turn to don't need to offer advice or tell you what to do step by step. They simply need to hold space and listen, empathizing with and validating your emotional feelings and giving you space to be brutally honest about your experience. Let them know you want them to ask challenging questions more than give detailed advice, and at times, that you'd like to hear how they've handled similar situations.

One of the challenges to finding this type of emotional support is that friends and family step into the role of the objective "listener." They may give advice and invalidate your pain, or just share their opinions rather than give you space to share what you need. As a word of caution, most people don't have experience in responding to a breakup in a productive, healthy way, so the advice you *do* receive is often impotent, needy, and can make the situation worse, yet it can be helpful to know other people have struggled too and you are not alone in your thoughts and feelings.

This is one of the reasons I'm such a big believer in coaching. I've worked with dozens of coaches over the course of my career. I can tell you from personal experience there's a sense of safety and emotional freedom from having someone whose only responsibility is to show up, listen, and ask tough questions to help you discover what's true for *you*—not what they believe the truth to be. Specifically, I encourage you to seek out a men's coach who specializes in relationships and breakups.

Over the past ten years, my team and I at Knowledge for Men have created one of the preeminent coaching experiences for men looking to reclaim their power, grow into their strongest selves, and create incredible romantic relationships that last. If after finishing this book you're interested in learning more and seeing if we're a good fit, you can submit an application for the program and schedule a discovery call with one of our coaches by visiting the link below:

knowledgeformen.com/grow

OPTIONAL COMMITMENT TO ACCELERATE RESULTS

Before concluding this section, I wanted to share one final action that can accelerate your results across each of the core commitments and put you on the fast track to rapid growth and recovery.

Exploring new environments (or optimizing your existing environment)

While I'm a big believer in the power of moving to new cities (or even countries) to accelerate your growth, expand your social circle, and break free from your comfort zone, I don't recommend that you take such a drastic action immediately post breakup.

The emotions from your breakup are still too high and there's no way for you to determine whether such a move aligns with your values and vision *or* if it's simply a way to escape. If you suddenly pack up and leave town *because* of your breakup, you're making this decision because of your ex. She's still in control and she still has power over you.

However, you can still apply this same principle in smaller ways. First, you could consider moving to a new place in your current city. If you and your ex lived together and your current place is filled with reminders of the times you shared together, this can be an especially effective way to begin reclaiming your lost identity after a breakup.

Spend some time thinking about the type of lifestyle you want, like the activities you want to do, the passions you want to explore, the people you want to surround yourself with. Start searching for places in nearby areas that are conducive to that lifestyle. As an important thought exercise, consider the type of lifestyle you'd want if you *knew* your ex was never coming back. Where would you want to be? How would you want to spend your days, evenings and weekends? Once you have your answer, do more research and put together a plan into moving somewhere that's aligned with what you discovered and actually go visit that location.

The second option, which is becoming easier than ever with the proliferation of remote work, is to take time to travel abroad and explore new countries as a part of your recovery strategy. This might seem unrealistic for many of you reading this, but with a little creative energy and research, it's very doable.

If you're stuck in a lease, you can consider subletting or using an online service to rent your place out while you travel. If you have car payments, there are sites that allow you to rent your car out and cover the monthly fees (and you can pay a friend or family member to handle logistics while you're gone).

If you have money saved up, you can travel on a budget to dozens of countries in Eastern Europe, Southeast Asia, and Latin America. You can travel like a king in these locations for a lot less than you think.

If traveling or moving to a new place isn't feasible, you can opt for the third option, reinventing your environment. Again, it's likely that your current environment is filled with reminders of your ex, reminders you're forced to confront on a daily basis. And if you spent a significant amount of time together, your home may be a reflection of your past relationship, not your new identity as a man. She may have helped you pick out furniture or curtains or paint colors. Every single item that holds the memory of your ex is yet another daily obstacle on your road to recovery.

So, if you're staying in your current place, use some of the money you're no longer spending on the relationship to renovate or reinvent your space. Paint the walls a new color. Get some new furniture. Rearrange the rooms. Even if you're on a budget, you can find simple ways to make your space feel like an authentic reflection of *you* and the man you're becoming. Adopting a minimalist lifestyle can be helpful and just help you purge a lot of unnecessary items.

I know this might sound simple, but I can't stress how powerful this is for accelerating your growth. When my ex left, the timing was fortuitous. My lease was expiring, and I had no other option than to find a new home. Even though I only moved a few miles away, the impact was immediate. The day I moved out of my old place and sold or donated half of everything I owned, I felt lighter, happier, and more free. Instead of spending every day being reminded of what I'd lost, I was better able to focus on the present and creating a new future.

Ultimately, that's the purpose of everything I've shared in this chapter. The past is the past. You can't go back and change it. And right now, your job is to boldly move forward with your new life, with or without your ex.

YOUR 90-DAY SPRINT TO FREEDOM

Now that you understand the core strategy that will allow you to recover and reclaim your power faster whether you want your ex back or not, the next step is simple: to codify your exact game plan for the next ninety days and review it every single day in the mornings and at night. Ideally, you want to have a coach or accountability partner you can check in with to ensure you're staying on track and taking the right actions to guarantee recovery.

Right now, I want you to write down the answers to the following questions:

1. **Health and Fitness**

   - What fitness plan am I going to follow to ensure I get into the best shape of my life to increase my confidence, attractiveness, and self-esteem?
   - What rules will I implement to fuel myself in a way that is healthy, sustainable, and gives me the energy I need to undertake these journeys?
   - How am I going to rest and recover to make sure I feel my best emotionally, physically, and psychologically?
   - What actions am I going to take this week to improve my appearance and how I feel about the way I'm showing up in the world?

2. **Professional Success**

   - What specific actions am I going to take to excel in my career?
   - What skill must I develop to make this a reality?
   - What is one bold risk I'm going to take or big dream I'm going to pursue?
   - What specific investment am I going to make in myself and my growth?
   - Who are the people who can help me achieve my financial and professional goals?

3. **Passions and Hobbies:**

   - What are some lost or new hobbies or passions I'm interested in pursuing?
   - What are the hobbies I'm committed to developing right now?
   - What is one social hobby I can develop to expand my network, develop interesting skills, and potentially meet new women?
   - How can I transfer my distracted time into "passion time" and continue exploring new ideas and growing as a man, even when I'm not actively engaged in a hobby or skill?

4. **Social Life & Support System**

- Who are the three people I've lost touch with who I'm going to reach out to today?
- What event will I begin hosting on a weekly or bi monthly basis? Who are three to five people I can invite today to get the ball rolling?
- Who are the people with whom I will not discuss my breakup?
- Who are the people I can trust to listen to my inner struggles?
- Do I need to enlist the support of a professional (therapist, counselor, or coach) to support me on my journeys for accountability and follow through on what matters most?

THE TWO FUTURES

I know this might seem like a lot. You might be tempted to cop out of this journey and hide behind the excuse that you "don't have time" to engage in these areas of your life. My challenge to you is to question this belief wholeheartedly.

What else are you doing right now that is more important than what we discussed? Just as importantly, once you've removed the demands of a full-time romantic relationship and the wasted time spent indulging in vices and distractions, you'll realize that you have more time than you think. The most important way to invest that time is by fully committing to the most important journeys in life that foster growth.

After my last breakup, I found myself going to bed at nine and waking up at six, ready to crush the day. When I removed endless TV marathons, social media binges, or debating politics with strangers online, I had almost too much time on my hands.

My business grew. I got into the best shape of my life. My social circle expanded. Women were approaching me and wanting to go out. My sense of aliveness, peace, and joy started to come back. Even though I've made a living in the personal development and peak performance space for nearly a decade, I achieved more than I thought I was capable of in less time because I channeled the intense energy of the breakup in productive ways.

And that's what I want for you. I want you to thrive, to grow, and to feel so excited and alive that you start to feel *grateful* for the breakup because it brought you back (or closer) to the man you always knew you could be. So, be honest with yourself about how you're spending your time now and consider the following:

"If I continue wasting my time on vices, distractions, and wallowing over my ex in despair, where will my life be in ninety days and how will I feel about myself?"

Then consider:

"If I commit to these journeys and go ALL IN on my life and dreams, where will my life be in ninety days and how will I feel about myself?"

Time will pass either way. The question real question is, "Who will I be when it passes?"

And the brutal truth is, you only have two options: progression or regression. There is no middle ground, no staying where you are. You either grow, improve, and get stronger, or fall into a downward spiral of negativity. It's a fundamental law of nature. You're either consciously fighting entropy in your life or you're a victim to it.

Women will respond to you with apathy, if they even respond at all. Your friends and social circle will slowly start to distance themselves from you because you aren't providing positive value, only leeching value by draining them and playing the victim.

Or you can choose the path of commitment and reinvention, using the pain you're experiencing as a reason to grow rather than an alibi for self-sabotage. It won't happen overnight, but as the weeks and months move forward, you'll slowly start to transform your life and think less and less about your ex.

The truth is you are the key variable that determines which reality comes to fruition. Both paths are hard. Both can be painful. But one leads to the promised land and the other to hell on earth.

So, which path will you choose?

BIG IDEAS:

1. **Ceasing contact only works if you fill the void wisely.**
   Ceasing contact with your ex is necessary, but not sufficient. Unless you find positive outlets to fill the void left in her absence, you will succumb to needy, chasing, weak behavior and unhealthy vices. This will push her further away and you'll fail to grow into the attractive man who can get her back or attract a new partner.

2. **Vices must be consciously controlled.**
   In an ideal world, you would be able to eliminate all vices outright after your breakup. But this is the *real* world. It's essential that you create clear constraints and parameters around these behaviors and enlist the help of an accountability partner, so you don't extend the breakup recovery process longer than necessary.

3. **Growth is the antidote to suffering.**
   The most effective way to overcome the pain of your breakup is by reinventing yourself and growing into a stronger, more attractive man, specifically in health and fitness, professional success, passions and hobbies, your social life, an emotional support system, and a new environment that fits your new identity.

   By progressing in these areas of life, you'll not only recover faster, you'll increase your value and transform who you are as a man. You'll live a richer, more enjoyable, and more fulfilling life, with or without your ex.

CHAPTER 5:

REWRITING THE STORY OF YOUR BREAKUP

After going through multiple breakups and coaching many men in the same position, I've discovered that there's one brutal truth men tend to ignore: the relationship wasn't as good as you think it was. If it was, it wouldn't have ended.

Too often, men glamorize their former relationships, ignoring the misalignment, problems, and toxicity that plagued them. Instead, they focus on isolated moments of bliss and harmony that existed far in the past. They confuse the pain of their loss with the alleged depth of their love (or biological need for sex).

This is not to say that your relationship was "bad," or that you and your ex didn't truly love each other and share positive memories together. Rather, during and after the separation, it's natural to lose touch with reality. Some men fail to acknowledge the truth about their relationship, or to see their former partner and the life they had through an objective lens.

Until the initial shock of the experience subsides, you can't see reality clearly and honestly assess the relationship you had for what it was. The truth is there are only two possibilities.

Either your relationship was the right fit for your life, or—for reasons that we'll explore throughout this chapter—it wasn't. In either case, the pain and emotional anguish you're experiencing are valid and true for you *right now*.

But the fact that you're experiencing pain because of your breakup does not mean you must reunite with your ex.

It doesn't mean that you're compatible or that your future will be better if you get her back. Your pain simply means you're a healthy, functioning human whose emotions function normally. You lost someone that you loved, and that loss hurts.

This chapter will address the emotional compulsions that can make the situation worse and unravel your fantasies about the relationship so you can discover what's best for you moving forward.

I'm not here to give you direct answers because every situation is different. I'm only going to help you ask yourself the right questions to uncover the truth and decide from a place of power, values, and abundance what winning in the future actually looks like.

THE FINAL COMMITMENT

During the early stages of my own breakup, I followed the commitments religiously. My friends and family were all impressed with my external successes and thought I was well on my way to getting over her.

But I was still hurting inside, especially at night and in the early mornings before I was fully awake. I would think about my ex in the middle of a set at the gym and have to hold back an emotional outburst. I'd enjoy a nice dinner with friends or family, then on the way home I'd be teary-eyed the entire drive. During a date once, the woman stopped in mid-conversation and asked me what was wrong because she could sense a deep sadness and lack of presence in me. My ex was on my mind and, despite my external growth with the core commitments, she continued to hold an invisible space in my thoughts and feelings deep inside, although on the outside you could never see it unless you knew me well.

Even though the core commitments created momentum and gave me a greater sense of self-esteem and confidence, there was still something missing that hindered my ability to fully heal and move forward. There was a final commitment that I hadn't yet recognized, a commitment to uncovering the truth about her and the relationship.

It wasn't until I began to question *her* value and look at the relationship with open eyes that her power over me and the obsession of her began to fade.

The core commitments are essential to the recovery process because without them, the pain will cannibalize your personal power, confidence, and self-worth. If you're stuck in a downward spiral and constantly thinking about your ex, the anxiety will build up and compulsions will follow, leading to desperate and often irreversible acts. Without healthier outlets, you'll reach out to her in this weak emotional state and push her further away and likely create humiliation for yourself. You'll revert back to the first, most painful stage of the breakup all over again, reducing all the progress you've made.

To prevent this, you must unpack the truth of your relationship and understand what you've really lost and what you've gained. Believe it or not, you've gained a tremendous amount even though it's hard to see and feel right now.

When you unpack this, you regain your power and shift your mindset from, "I miss her so much, life is not the same without her and I want her back," to "Maybe this breakup is the best thing that could of happened to me." It is this very epiphany that allows for the next stage of recovery to unfold.

This is not to say that you should or should not get your ex back. It is simply a sign of growth when you are able to find the opportunity within the obstacle, to grow into a stronger man and better lover, regardless of who that next partner will be.

This thought process is more attractive and increases your value. It replaces the belief that this one person is the only source of love, intimacy, and connection and you've lost it forever. That belief is false, and you must break the negative thought cycle and focus on the uncomfortable truth instead of the comfortable mind-made fantasy that soothes your anxiety.

A word of caution: if you're desperately reading this book cover to cover in a heightened state of emotion, the pain may still be too intense to get the most value out of this next section. If you're still in the early stage of implementing the core commitments, it may take several weeks for the emotional shock and pain to subside enough to be honest with your answers.

The state in which you enter this phase of deep introspection will determine the answers you uncover, which will dictate your actions moving forward.

If you're in a highly anxious, needy, and desperate state and the pain of the breakup is so debilitating that you can't think about anything but her, your answers will reflect this. The last thing you want to do is take action based on weak answers that are likely to make the situation worse. You won't be able to see her or the relationship clearly, and every attempt to uncover the truth will be sabotaged by your intense desire to get her back out of scarcity.

However, if you're following the core commitments and building greater momentum, and you're experiencing more confidence and self-esteem, you'll be in a better state of emotional stability. You can at least *begin* to see reality through an objective lens and uncover the truth. From this state, you can unravel the past and use what you discover to guide you toward a greater future.

You'll probably want to revisit the following section and the questions in it every week for the first month or so of this process. Every time you answer these questions, the pain will lessen, and the reality of your relationship will become clearer. It won't happen overnight, but with persistence, you'll arrive at the truth.

Before we dive in, allow me to be frank. As you're reading this section and answering the questions, it may feel like I'm discouraging you from pursuing a future with your ex, but that's not my intention. To reclaim your power, you must first remove her from the pedestal.

If you don't challenge her value, understand the opportunity cost of being with her versus new women, and question whether or not she is the right fit for your future, you're going to fail.

I'm not here to diminish her, but to humanize her to a level that's equal to yours. All too often, men idolize their ex after a breakup, portraying her as some perfect, infallible goddess who was single-handedly responsible for all of the joy, pleasure, and happiness in his life. Not only is this frame ridiculous, but it feeds into weak, regretful, and humiliating behaviors that are guaranteed to stunt your progress and keep you trapped in a fantasy.

By submitting your ex and your relationship through a ruthless examination, you'll be able to remove her from the pedestal and decide how you want to proceed from a place of power, values, and abundance. That's a far healthier place for all relationships to begin instead of one of weakness, desperation, and scarcity.

There isn't a single woman on the planet who would pass all the following "tests" you're about to read. All of us are imperfect human beings doing the best we can with what we know at the time. Relationships take commitment and work… period. The question is simply, "Is she the person I want to do this work with, and who will do it equally with me?"

TURN THE TABLES: APPLY THE ATTRACTION EQUATION ON HER

In the first section of this book, I shared the concept of the "Attraction Equation." To recap, a man's attractiveness to his partner is equal to the value he provides minus the value he takes or his neediness.

Attraction = Value - Neediness

You've already filtered your own behaviors and actions through this equation, so now it's time to turn the tables and consider your ex's true attractiveness.

I'm going to share some questions I asked myself during my breakup. Once I started to understand what was *really* happening in my relationship and what I'd really lost when it ended, it was a major turning point in my healing and recovery, let alone in regaining my power.

IDENTIFY HER TRUE VALUE

One of the first steps to get closer to the truth about your relationship is to consider the tangible value she provided in your life. For most men, this can be accomplished with four simple questions:

1. Was she meeting your core needs in the relationship? Or was it like pulling teeth every time you expressed your needs to her?
2. Was she an asset or a liability in your life? If she was an asset in some areas and a liability in others, then identify which was greater and if it was off balance?
3. Did she support or hinder your personal and professional growth? (If the answer is no, this cannot be ignored.)
4. Is she enabling or preventing you from living the life you want?

The above questions should give you the sense of direction so listen to your gut. So now that you have a general idea of her true value, here are additional questions to further examine if you are still on the fence:

1. Beyond sex, enjoyable company, and fun times together, how did being with her increase your quality of life and fulfill needs that would be difficult to meet by another partner?
2. If you take away the possibility of sex, would going on a 10 day vacation with her excite you or bore you?
3. Did she support your growth as a man emotionally, intimately, sexually, or financially to help you achieve your goals?
4. Did she support and challenge you to level up when you were feeling beaten down, complacent, and tired?
5. Did she bring value to your social circle and understand that time away from her with friends and colleagues was beneficial to your growth?
6. Did she help you live a healthy lifestyle or unhealthy lifestyle?

7. What was her relationship with tobacco, drugs, and alcohol, and what was its impact on you?
8. Was she growing personally, professionally, and emotionally in her own life or was she a lost soul aimlessly going through life chasing status and pleasure?
9. Did she communicate and handle conflict effectively, or did she hide and later have a sudden emotional outburst?
10. Were you building an incredible life together or *were you building an incredible for her?*

Once you've gotten the specific and tangible ways she provided value in your life—you should be able to write down several examples for everything you identified—the next question is how much value did she *take* in exchange for this? Was this a negative, equal, or positive value exchange?

Every relationship requires compromises and tradeoffs. It's part of sharing your life with another human being. The problem is in most dysfunctional relationships, the tradeoffs take more value than they provide for far too long. As long as they're having semi-regular orgasms and there aren't fighting, most men never stop to ask themselves if this relationship is even serving them or if they are just holding onto something out of scarcity and comfort.

Once you're clear on the value that she provided, take a few minutes to get clear on the *cost* in explicit detail.

1. What did your ex need financially in exchange for the value she provided?
2. Did she expect lavish date nights, expensive gifts, and exotic trips more than you liked to support or felt she deserved?
3. Did you handle her personal bills—car payments, phone bills, insurance, taxes, etc—even if you were struggling with your own finances?
4. On an average month, how much of your income went to her, either directly or indirectly, to maintain the relationship?

5. Would you rather take all that money and energy and put it into yourself or invest it in valuable assets? Or do you honestly feel it was a worthwhile investment in the relationship?

Next, consider this. How much time was required from you to maintain the relationship? While every relationship dynamic is unique and spending quality time together is an essential part of any relationship, many men will invest *more* time than they want in their partner at the expense of their own pursuits, goals, and well-being.

A good way to frame this question is to ask yourself, "How many hours each week did I feel *pressured* to spend time with my partner even though I wanted to do something else?"

1. Did you regularly miss out on "guys' nights," say no to trips you wanted to take that she couldn't join, abandon your hobbies in favor of another couch-cuddle Netflix binge, or feel like you had to quit work early—even when you didn't want to—so that you could make it home in time to spend the entire evening with her?
2. Can you think of any specific examples where you wanted to do something fun or exciting but decided not to because you felt like you had to spend that time with her?
3. How much energy did the relationship take from you compared to how much energy it *gave* to you?
4. Was there a high level of drama that caused you to feel like you were constantly walking on eggshells?
5. Were her parents, family or even extended family a lot to handle and show up for?
6. Did you feel like a parent in the relationship who was responsible for your partner's emotional state and quality of life?
7. Did her emotional neediness leave you feeling drained and constantly on guard because the smallest mistake or wrong word sent her spiraling into a hyperemotional state?
8. Write down all of the specific situations you can think of where her emotional needs reduced the freedom you felt to be yourself and live on your terms.

Once you're clear on both sides of the equation, the final question arises. I want you to clearly define the quality of life return you achieved for the investments (time, energy, money, stress, well-being) you made in her. You might go through this exercise and realize that she *did* provide more value than she took. But the question then becomes, how *much* more value?

In my coaching experience, relationships that last provide at least twice as much value as they take. According to research from the Gottman Institute, a company that specializes in relationship psychology and has a track record of predicting divorces with 92% accuracy, healthy long-lasting relationships have on average five or more positive interactions for every one negative interaction. If you're struggling to clearly define the value exchange in your relationship, ask yourself, "Was I experiencing significantly more positive experiences than negative experiences?" Please do not think "okay" are positive experiences. That's not enough.

When you're honest with yourself about these questions, the answers may surprise you.

THE BIG "WHYS"

Once you're clear on the explicit value exchange of your previous relationship, there are three questions you must ask yourself that will reveal critical truths about your relationship *and* yourself.

1. Why did I start this relationship?
2. Why did I stay in this relationship?
3. Why would I want her back?

If the amount of value that she provided was more than the amount of value she took, the answer to all three questions will be clear cut. She made your life better or she did not.

More often than not, the answers to these questions reveal uncomfortable truths about ourselves. They shine a light on the demons lurking in our psyches that we've been unable or unwilling to acknowledge and work through. Honestly answering these questions could be one of the most eye-opening exercises in this entire book.

When you consider why you entered the relationship in the first place, I want you to think back to the stage of life you were in when the relationship started.

In my case, I'd recently lost my father and a close friend in the same month. I had ended a four-year relationship. I'd been dealing with an exhausting health battle that included chronic fatigue, headaches, and brain fog, all of which led to one of the darkest valleys of my entire life. I thought I knew depression before, but this was on a whole other level I'd never experienced.

Then, I met a woman who brought me a tremendous amount of joy, aliveness, and adventure. Because her presence helped me get out of the pain and trauma I'd been feeling, I overlooked the red flags that would have been a deal breaker had I been healthy and emotionally strong.

During that season, I placed a higher premium on the fun nights, new experiences, and adventures than I did on my deeper relationship values of shared growth and authentic communication. As I started to heal from my own pain, the value I was getting began to diminish. The red flags became more obvious, and I became more disengaged and disconnected from her.

As a result of our incompatibility, the value *I* provided to her began to decrease as I pulled away emotionally, even if I was physically still with her. Instead of fully loving and accepting her as she was, I felt compelled to force growth and progress in her life to help her catch up to "my level," causing her to feel unaccepted and unloved. Ultimately, this caused a drop in emotional attraction, which ended the relationship. When emotional attraction drops, there is low motivation to show up and resolve issues, and leaving the relationship is the eventual outcome.

By understanding the season of life in which you entered the relationship, you may better understand why you ignored red flags that later became more apparent with time, or that you two simply outgrew the relationship and each other.

She may have met your needs *then*, but she did not grow into the type of partner who could meet the needs you have *now*. And that's okay.

It doesn't mean that either of you failed, only that your relationship served a purpose for a phase in both of your lives and then came to completion.

Take some time to write out a brief overview of what phase of life you were in months before meeting your ex. What were your important values when you met compared to what they are today? What was your emotional state? What were your needs and desires? What challenges were you experiencing personally, spiritually and professionally?

Once you understand the state that you entered the relationship in, you'll be better equipped to understand why you began a relationship with her, why the disconnect began, and why you stayed with her for as long as you did.

Some men stay in a relationship because it's the only thing they know. They've experienced few other women or other relationships and they're operating out of fear and scarcity. They worry that, if they lose this relationship, they'll lose their only source of love, connection, and sex. Maybe they're unhappy with themselves and who they are, so they feel crippled by the thought of being alone, having to meet new women and go on a dating journey. They've never fully committed to the journey of creating an abundant dating life, so they live in fear that this is the best they'll ever have and fear the unknown.

For many, they stay in a relationship because they're a victim of something called the sunk cost fallacy. They've already worked so hard at the relationship that their lives are intertwined logistically. They made so many commitments—even children or marriage—that they don't want to look like a failure by admitting that the relationship no longer serves them. They may even feel selfish for doing so. They don't want to be "wrong" about their past actions and choices, so they continue sinking their time, energy and resources into a relationship that doesn't meet their needs or improve their quality of life. It's like holding onto a stock that has now become a penny stock and hoping for the Hail Mary "comeback".

The pain of starting over with a new relationship feels greater than the pain of staying in a relationship that isn't working. As a result, they settle for certain pain over uncertain growth.

For others still, their relationship is a crutch. It's a form of escape that they use to avoid facing the pain and problems in other areas of their life. They entered into the relationship from a needy, desperate frame where they had so many challenges: their job sucks, their health sucks, their social life sucks, their level of adventure sucks, their lifestyle sucks.

Therefore, they enter and continue a relationship because it feels like the only good thing in their life. It's all they have that brings them some form of aliveness and escape from the reality of their fractured life. Without their partner, life is empty and meaningless. This is often the most painful truth to admit because the moment you do, you can't run and hide from those parts of yourself anymore. Even if she came back tomorrow, you'd know deep down that she isn't really good for you any longer. You're in pain, and you're using her as a bandage to cover the deeper problems you've ignored for too long.

Note: If you don't resonate with this, and your overall life is good, then you have deeper self-esteem, confidence and self-worth issues with women. You likely lack a strong history of dating quality women in your past and you are clinging on to what you have out of fear that this is the best you can attract in your life. But you are not the same man you are today that you were 5, 10, 20 years ago. Today, you are capable of so much more than you could possibly know if you commit to the journey of success with women, self-love and freedom of self-expression. See The Dating Playbook for Men on amazon as an ideal next step for you.

Can you see how this weak frame can come across as needy and reduce your value and attraction? The relationship was based on nothing more than needing her to fill a void instead of loving her for who she is and showing up fully for her.

Finally, once you've gained more clarity on why you started the relationship and why you stayed, an important question to consider is: Why would you want her back?

We'll continue to unpack this question throughout the rest of this chapter. But for now, if you want your ex back, I want you to take a few minutes to clarify *why* you want her back in explicit detail, while removing sex, comfort, and familiarity from your response.

What is the unique value that she provides that makes you believe she is a great value add to your life? And is this greater than finding another woman who's potentially more aligned with your values and vision? When you look back on all of the ways that she extracted value from your life, are you willing to accept them and continue to live with them knowing that these may only increase with time? If absolutely nothing about her behavior or character changed if you got back together, would you still want her back? Is this a long term win or a short term fix?

Most importantly, why are you convinced that she's the right person for you (both today and in the future) despite the pain she's recently caused and the unresolved problems you had?

DOUBTS AND RESERVATIONS

Allow me to be frank, your relationship had major challenges even during the glory days. What were your doubts and reservations about her in the long term? Were there any red flags you overlooked because she met specific needs during a specific season of your life?

Just because a relationship wasn't overtly toxic or dysfunctional, that doesn't mean you should commit to it for life.

It doesn't mean that she was compatible with you as a long-term partner. Many relationships are meant to exist only for a season of life, whether that's months, years, or even decades. People come through your life, add value, then move on. Fighting against this is at the root of your emotional suffering.

If you're honest with yourself, were there any character traits or behaviors that made you doubt the long-term potential of the relationship? Were there specific red flags that you acknowledged but chose to ignore?

For example:

- Did she party too frequently or abuse drugs and alcohol in a way that could have become problematic over time?

- Did she have a traumatic past, such as abuse, abandonment, or toxic relationship patterns, that she wasn't actively working to resolve through therapy, coaching, or other healing practices?

- Did she criticize you in front of other people or personally attack you during arguments and conflicts, making it difficult to resolve issues?

- Did she have poor self-esteem and rely on you for constant validation that she was "good enough" as a woman?

- Did she violate your boundaries despite you communicating your expectations?

- Did she lack the ability to regulate her own emotions and expect you to soothe her every time she got upset, or lash out at you over problems that you didn't cause?

- Were you misaligned on important values like having kids, money, or location, and did you decide to compromise on things that mattered to you just to make her happy? (There will be more on this later.)

Now consider what your relationship would have been like five or ten years from now if these doubts or red flags were never resolved. What too many men fail to realize is that often "what you see is what you get." Unless she has a strong growth mindset and desire for change on her own, it's unlikely that she will change in the ways that you precisely want. With time, the problems you experienced would likely have gotten worse, the red flags more prominent, the incompatibility driving a deeper wedge.

Once you understand this, you have to ask yourself this question:

Even if you have the opportunity to get her back in the future, can you love her fully for who she is *today*, knowing that she may never change? Or was your love contingent on her becoming an idealized version of herself that exists only in your mind?

A trap that many men fall into, one that I've fallen into myself, is treating their partner like a problem to be solved. But a healthy partnership doesn't require you to "solve" your partner. It requires that you're both committed to growing and solving your own problems, showing up as two individually healthy people and using your relationship as a container to facilitate growth, connection and intimacy.

THE MALE EGO AND WINNING

The male ego loves to "win." It loves to be the knight in shining armor who rides in and saves the day in the face of adversity. But in a relationship, this natural hardwiring can be a recipe to losing her permanently.

Long lasting relationships aren't about winning, being right or boosting your ego. They're about coming together and creating a greater quality of life than they could have on their own. Together, they are more powerful, abundant and alive. They are not pulling each other down or creating barriers to living the life they want.

All too often, men knowingly stay in relationships that aren't a good fit because they don't want to lose.

They believe that if the relationship ends, they've lost. They're a failure as a man. A failure to their family, to their peers and social community. So, they do everything in their power to try and "fix" their partner and turn her into the type of person that they can love (from a place of disapproval) instead of simply loving her for who she is (approval).

When I reflect on some of my previous relationships, this dynamic was apparent during the last few months we spent together. I had my doubts. I knew that my needs weren't being met. But my ego wanted to win, even if winning meant being with someone who wasn't the best fit for my future. Isn't that losing?

I wanted to prove to myself that I could make things work and wasn't someone who fails in relationships. But because of this frame, I withheld the love and affection that she deserved in the present and focused my attention and energy on "fixing" both her and the relationship, in hopes I could "win" yet another challenge.

Once I became aware of this pattern, I realized that even though I did love and care for her, much of the compulsion I felt to "win her back" didn't come from a place of authentic love, values, and connection. It was my ego at work.

This can be just as true even if you weren't trying to play the "parent" or force your partner to become the person you want them to be. Maybe there were fundamental incompatibilities in the relationship, but you didn't want to admit it. Maybe you realized that you'd outgrown the relationship, but you didn't want to lose the years of hard work and energy, money, and emotional resources you'd already invested in the relationship. Maybe your family and friends expressed concerns about the relationship or had doubts that the two of you would last but you didn't listen to them, only because you felt like ending the relationship would mean that you'd lost. They were right, you were wrong, but your big messy failure would be on display for everyone to see. Perhaps you had a boring sex life that lacked passion and intimacy, but she showed up well in other areas that mattered to you And on the outside looking in it appears that you have a great relationship, so your ego wants to keep the relationship together to avoid social and familial disappointment.

When our ego is bruised and we're faced with an unexpected loss, it's easy to conflate a blow to our pride with a strong desire for reconciliation. So, my question to you is simple: Do you want her back because she was genuinely a good fit for your life and future? Or do you want her back because your ego can't stand losing and you're fixated on solving problems?

(MIS)ALIGNED AND SETTLING FOR COMFORT

One of the unique challenges of relationships is that compromise is necessary. But when does compromise go too far? All too often, I see men who sacrifice the things that are most meaningful to them for the sake of making a relationship work.

One or two small sacrifices won't break a relationship, especially if they're appreciated and reciprocated. But over time, every unrequited compromise will breed resentment and frustration. When you think about the big things that make a relationship last, it's important to consider whether or not the two of you were aligned to begin with.

- Did you both agree on the things that mattered most to each other?
- What were her core values? What were yours?
- What did she expect from you as a partner? Did you feel like her expectations aligned with what you were willing to give?
- What did you expect from her? Did she meet your expectations or not?
- Did the two of you agree about big life decisions like marriage, raising children, roles in the household, and where you wanted to live?
- Did you both get along with and enjoy spending time with each other's families?
- Did you share similar beliefs and behaviors around spending and saving money?
- Did you share similar values and behaviors around being healthy?
- Did you meet each other's needs sexually and romantically?

One of the biggest challenges in relationships is that you love someone so much that you want them to change to fit into your ideal version of a partner so that you can love them even more. Instead of loving them for who they are today, you love them for who they *could* be tomorrow. If you both share this vision of your ideal selves and she legitimately wants to grow in the ways that you value–*and vice versa*–this can be a beautiful dynamic. You're able to support each other in your pursuits of fully realizing your potential, and you're aligned on what it looks like to be your "best selves."

But if you have different visions, it creates an awfully toxic dynamic. Neither of you can fully love or accept the other because you're constantly trying to change each other. If she wants to live a simple and quiet life but you want her to be a hard-charging "boss woman," neither of you can win. Maybe she wants to grow, but she doesn't want to grow in the ways that *you* want her to grow.

Inversely, if she enjoys being a hard-working overachiever but you want her to be the loving wife who's emotionally available at night and happy to run the household while you make the money, you're setting yourselves up for failure. It's not because either one of you are wrong, but because you have needs and desires that aren't aligned.

When both of you have different versions of "ideal partner," the only two options you have are to *separate* or *settle*.

Either you accept that you aren't right for each other because you want different things, or you settle for living a life that isn't aligned with your deepest desires. You end up sharing that life with a partner you'll never fully accept and who will never fully accept you. Both options are painful, yet one is more painful over time. The pain of separation is temporary, the pain of settling lasts a lifetime.

THE VALUE OF YOUR FREEDOM

Since 1775, more than 1,354,000 American men and women have given their lives in the defense of a single idea. This idea has ignited revolutions around the world, toppled tyrannical governments, and taken the human species to unseen heights.

Freedom.

Yet every day, hundreds of millions—if not billions—of people willingly sacrifice their own freedoms because often they're afraid of being alone. They give up their most valuable resources: their time, energy and money to feel secure, certain, and safe. *What's your freedom worth to you?*

The price of being in a relationship that isn't a resounding "hell yes!" goes beyond the obvious cost of not dating or having experiences with other women. It even goes beyond the time, energy, and money spent meeting her needs and maintaining the relationship because the relationship doesn't *just* include you and her. It includes everyone in her world that you are required to show up for, like her friends, family, and co-workers.

It means sacrificing holidays and weekends with *your* family to spend time with hers. It means saying no to invites and social events with your circle to spend time with her friends (people you may not even like). It means not traveling to the places you'd love to experience to accommodate her ideas of travel. It means using your hard-earned resources to support her in her goals instead of going all-in on your own.

Being in a relationship fundamentally alters the trajectory of both lives. It can place limits on both of your abilities to focus on yourselves, your growth, and your own goals—basically, the core commitments. It imposes limitations on the types of experiences you can have and the lifestyles you can live or dream of living.

But as some of you might think, this isn't a call to eschew romantic relationships in favor of the single life. Rather, it's a call to fully realize what's at stake by first understanding the value of your freedom.

The brutal truth is that when you look at their actions, the masses of men *don't* value and fully exercise their freedom. Because they value it so little, it can be terrifying when it's forced on them by a breakup. They don't know what to do with it, so they view it instead as loneliness, uncertainty, and loss. They end up disregarding the incredible experiences and adventures that await them if they choose to open their eyes.

If man does not know what to do with his newfound freedom, he will suffer far more than the man who uses his freedom productively post-breakup.

The hours of 5:00pm to 10:00pm will be some of your most challenging hours if you don't know what to do with your freedom. You'll be more likely to succumb to unhealthy vices and distractions since this was time you would have spent with her. A man who does not value his own freedom is needy and desperate, so he's quick to fight for the safety of the past. Ultimately, it's this devaluation of a man's own freedom that leads to the weak, needy, and low-value behaviors behind many breakups and divorces.

When a man understands the value of his freedom and the precious gift of living a self-reliant and self-generated life, he's living in his power. He knows that life on his own terms can be so inspiring, exciting, and joyful that he's unwilling to settle. From this place, he'll only enter into a relationship with a partner who is a "hell yes," someone who is more aligned with his values, visions, and desires, someone who magnifies his life.

Think about this same value proposition through the lens of a career. Imagine you were offered a job where you had to work 100-hour weeks every week for an entire year. Your entire life would center around this job and your freedom to go on adventures, travel, be with friends, and explore hobbies would be eliminated. Your compensation for sacrificing an entire year of your life would only be $50,000.

For most men, this offer would be an obvious "hell no." If they were going to sacrifice *that* much of their lives, they would demand compensation that made it worth their time. And yet many of you reading this right now have sacrificed years or even decades of your lives for a relationship that offered value far lower than what you were giving into it.

Strong, powerful, Grounded Men understand that their freedom is precious. It's the lifeblood of their masculine spirit and they protect it with their lives. They understand the value of what they have. If they're going to release it, it's only because they're getting something of great value in return.

The bottom line is that if you're with the right partner, relationships can be one of the most rewarding, enjoyable, and fulfilling parts of life. But if you choose to settle and sacrifice your freedom quickly to end your loneliness even if it's the wrong person, it can be a living hell and cost you years of your finite life.

So, I invite you to take full ownership of your newfound freedom. Claim it. Revel in it. And if you're going to let it go, ensure it's for a true win-win relationship.

A NET POSITIVE EXPERIENCE

In the business world, there's a single formula that determines the difference between a successful company and bankruptcy:

Revenue - Expenses = Profits.

The single-most important metric of a healthy business is how much net profit is left after all expenses and costs are paid. What does the owner walk away with free and clear?

For example, let's say you run a business selling watches online. You sell each watch for $100, and they cost you $25 to make, $25 to market, and $25 per unit to pay your team. That means you have $75 in expenses and you generate $25 in net profit.

Almost anyone who was able to repeat this process one hundred times a day would be thrilled by the result. He'd be generating $2,500 a day in income (almost $1M a year) despite $7,500 a day in expenses.

They wouldn't look at their expenses and be sad about all of the money they were "losing." Instead, they'd simply look at the bottom of their profit and loss sheet and see the thousands of dollars in profit they were earning every day as a direct result of their high expenses. Even though the expenses are greater, they're ultimately irrelevant. At the end of the day, the company is net positive, and the owner is on the fast track to success.

Now, imagine if the same owner only focused on the expenses. Without understanding that his business was net positive, he'd quickly fall into despair and consider bankruptcy. After all, he's spending almost $3 million a year in expenses! But he's only looking at half the picture. He's focusing on his losses rather than celebrating his gains.

This same principle is at play in your life right now. After a breakup, most men are focused only on their "expenses." All of their time, energy, and attention is centered around what they've lost. They magnify much of their suffering because they aren't opening their eyes to the complete picture.

Yes, breakups are painful. And yes, some levels of pain and suffering are an inevitable part of the process. Loss, struggle, and hardship are a part of the human experience. But in every loss, there is an even greater opportunity for the men who are willing to seize it.

What most men fail to realize is that there are two sides to their breakup. On the one side is everything they've lost: the love of a specific woman, intimate experiences, a source of connection and sex. On the other side is all they've gained and stand to gain by fully committing to themselves and their new life: invaluable lessons, freedom, professional growth, new friendships, better health, new adventures, the ability to experience new women guilt-free, the chance to pursue a higher quality and more aligned partner when the time is right. Mark my words, nearly everything that your ex provided to you is replaceable.

But it's up to you to claim this experience. You have to accept that the loss of your lover is simply the expense that had to be paid to realize the emotional, spiritual, professional, and personal "profits" that are waiting on the other side of this experience if you take full ownership of your post breakup experience.

So, my invitation to you is simple: shift your focus from what you've lost to what you've gained. Consider everything that can now come to fruition and everything you could now accomplish if you take this journey of recovery and personal reinvention seriously. If you do this, you'll quickly realize that—as painful as it may be right now—what you're experiencing today is ultimately one of the greatest gifts you've ever received.

ACCEPTING THE LAW OF NATURE

One of the greatest challenges a man faces after a painful breakup or divorce isn't the loss of love, the changes in his routine, or the challenge of finding a new partner.

It's the feeling of inadequacy as a man that arises from "failing" to make the relationship work.

After the breakup, we lambast ourselves for being unable to lead the relationship as the man we would like to have been. We regret how we fell into complacency and took her for granted when she was right next to you. We're angry with ourselves for failing to satisfy the needs and desires she expressed.

Yet even if you were "perfect" and met all of her needs, the law of nature is change. There was nothing you could have done to prevent the change of another person or their changing world.

You accept that the sun will rise and set. You accept that the days will grow warmer and brighter in the summer and colder and darker in the winter. You accept that your body and face will age with time. You may dislike these facts of life, but in the end, you accept them because you know there's no point in arguing or complaining against nature. All that's left for you is to accept, adapt, and move forward.

Every day, millions of men end relationships they believed would last. In many cases, the relationships were good, great even. Sometimes, the blame lies with the man, other times with his partner, and sometimes there's no one to blame at all. The relationship simply served its purpose in their lives and then ended.

All this situation says about you is that you are a human being going through a distinctly human experience. To recover from and grow through this experience, you must learn to accept it because change is a part of life. To resist change is to resist life. To resist life is to suffer.

Yet in your relationship, you're resisting the change you are experiencing right now. You're resisting the fact that people, emotions, and desires change with time. You're quick to blame yourself or judge your experience as "bad" instead of understanding that it's simply the law of nature.

In the ocean, when you're caught in a rip current, you can't fight it. The harder you try, the faster you tire out, and the more likely you are to drown. To survive, you must remain calm, allow yourself to float on the water, and then swim parallel to the beach to escape. This is nature, and it's the same way you must respond to the emotional rip current of your relationship.

One of the interesting quirks of the human mind is how our illusion of choice and free will colors our experience. When change happens in our life by choice, we view it as an opportunity because we believe we're in the driver's seat. When we quit a job, move to a new city, or end a relationship by choice, we feel less fearful and uncertain because we believe we're in control.

Yet when the same exact change happens by chance—or by someone else's choice—we view it as a crisis. We often focus exclusively on the perceived danger. We feel a loss of control and certainty about our future. And because we're unprepared, we're more fearful and anxious. Even though the same possibilities and opportunities exist as if we had experienced the change by choice, we fail to see them and thus fail to have joy and excitement for the future.

The beauty of any crisis is that it gives us an opportunity to come alive. You're more alert, more aware and more awake. Your senses are fully heightened in every moment. From this state, you have a choice. You can either channel every emotion productively into the core commitments and important journeys of life, or you can channel it destructively. Attempting to sedate the fear of danger and uncertainty with vices and distractions will mean prolonging your recovery process, making you more likely to do something humiliating in a desperate attempt to get your ex back.

Nothing is permanent in nature; there is either growth or decay. You're either growing closer to your partner or growing apart. You're growing into the man you want to be or decaying into a shell of your potential.

My invitation, as always, is to choose growth.

EMBRACE AMOR FATI

After learning to accept the changes in your life rather than resisting them, there's one final step before fully embracing the journey ahead of you. After accepting your breakup and all of the challenges that come with it, can you learn to *love* it?

Enter "*amor fati*," a Latin phrase meaning "a love of one's fate."

To love one's fate does not mean to find joy or bliss in the pains and trials of life like a masochist, but rather to love the *journey* of one's life as a whole. It requires you to see every pain and challenge as an opportunity for growth, to believe that everything—no matter how senseless it may seem or heart wrenching it may feel—is happening *for* you, not *to* you. It means you must accept that loss, suffering, and pain are necessary pit stops on the journey to self-actualization and to see them as a gift that enables you to look forward with enthusiasm to what awaits on the other side. Because if you embrace *amor fati*, it *is* a gift.

Ultimately, at the heart of this philosophy is the belief that nothing in life is good or bad. It is the meaning and story you ascribe to it that makes it so. The question for you then is:

Can you love this experience?

Your gut response may be to scream a resounding "no," to think I'm crazy for even *suggesting* that you could "love" the pain you're experiencing. And if that's where you are right now, I get it.

But when you step back and view your situation through an objective lens, you'll soon realize that the opportunities and potential ahead of you are immense. You've been given a clean slate to start anew. You have an opportunity to use this journey as fuel to architect a life of your choosing with less restraint. You get to enjoy the complete freedom of being a single man, traveling whenever and wherever you want, investing in whatever resources or adventures you want, and saying "yes" or "no" to whatever experiences are presented to you without having to check in with anyone.

You have the opportunity to experience new partners and become a more masterful lover, to pause, reflect, and reconsider the way you are choosing to live your life—casting away that which doesn't serve you and moving toward that which does. Regardless of how you choose to use this new opportunity, you must realize that this *is* an opportunity.

If you're resisting this idea, struggling to feel excited by the future and pining over what you've lost for months post breakup, then your vision isn't bigger than your past life. You must create a vision for the future so exciting that it sends tingles down your spine at the very thought of it. If even 15% of it came true it still supersedes your past life.

Remember, beyond the laws of physics and basic morality, there are no rules anymore. There are no restrictions on what you can do, who you can become, or who you can share your experiences with. You can write your own rules and design an exciting future that excites you.

What are the things you always wanted to do? The adventures you wanted to have? The experiences you crave the most? Journal your answers and then *start taking action towards those things*. It's likely that you now have more resources—time, money, and energy—so use them and get busy creating. Make this breakup worth it. Your future self needs you to.

CERTAIN AND UNCERTAIN FUTURES

One of the greatest challenges facing men today is overcoming the drive to settle for *certain* pain over *uncertain* growth. This compulsion can be present in any area of our lives. All too often, we'll settle for something that doesn't serve us or that is objectively toxic because we're fearful of the unknown.

We stay in a job because it feels safe and comfortable, even though we hate it. We stay in the same town where we grew up or finished college even though it impedes our progress and keeps us trapped. We stay in relationships that are dysfunctional or misaligned with our core values.

The problem with this line of thinking is that it's short sighted. No matter how painful our reality is, it's often more comfortable to settle for what we know than to courageously pursue what we truly desire. In the immediate future, you'll experience less pain by accepting your current reality. But what happens when we fast-forward?

We have a choice. It's a choice between the pain of regret and the pain of action. The pain of action weighs ounces and it's what people will remember you for, whereas the pain of regret weighs tons and gets buried with you.

Now that you've got more clarity on your previous relationship, I want you to consider what your future could look like if you get her back. If the value exchange you identified earlier stayed the same, are you investing your time, energy, and financial resources in a winning or losing asset? How would this value exchange impact your social, professional, sexual, and personal life? Would your quality of life be greater or lower if you stayed with her instead of pursuing different women, women who are more aligned with your values? Or would you be better off embracing intentional solitude for a season of your life?

Think about this famous quote from George Santayana: *"Those who cannot remember the past are condemned to repeat it."*

Your partner and relationship will be more or less the same as they were before the breakup. So, ask yourself, "Do I want to settle and repeat history, or write a new empowering story for my future?"

REPLACEMENT OR RECONCILIATION?

As I processed my pain, I began to realize that even though I loved my ex dearly and cherished the memories we shared together, she wasn't "the one" to spend the rest of my life with.

I knew that we were misaligned on important values and beliefs. But she'd met needs that were severely lacking at the time. Even though I knew this when we separated and had it written down multiple times in my journal, I ignored all logic and still wanted to see her again. At times, I felt compelled to chase her, to beg her to return, and I fantasized about what having her back would be like. Thankfully, I held onto those core commitments and uncovered the truth about the relationship, which kept this compulsion under control.

Then one day while sitting in traffic, reflecting on my breakup, I had an honest conversation with myself.

Me: "If you knew that you could have a better relationship with a higher-quality woman who met your needs and more, would you still want your ex back and be in this much pain?"

A split second later, I knew the answer.

Also Me: "No."

Then I continued.

Me: "Be really honest, Andrew, how hard would it be to replace her and find someone better? And how long would that take?"

Also Me: "six months or so, with focused effort."

Then I thought some more.

Me: "So this is really just about not wanting to go on a new journey into the unknown, and choosing familiar over unfamiliar?"

By reflecting on these gut-wrenching questions, I realized that the pain I was experiencing, although it was "real" to me, was being greatly exaggerated by my emotional state. When I looked at the situation objectively, the truth was, I hadn't lost as much as I'd gained. I'd received the opportunity to take invaluable lessons from the relationship and carry them into a new relationship that would be better aligned with the life I wanted.

That had been my ex's purpose, and it was served. I appreciate her for that role, and this understanding was an effective way to alleviate both my pain and my negative thoughts towards her.

While the answers to these questions will be different for every man, I want you to spend some time sitting with them and answering them honestly. If you were to fully commit to the dating journey and make finding a high-quality woman your priority for the next six months (while also becoming the type of man who could attract her), what would happen?

(NOTE: If you don't think this is possible, I encourage you to check out my bestseller, *The Dating Playbook for Men* on amazon, where I share an in-depth, step-by-step strategy to meet and attract your dream partner.)

Remember, there was a time in your life when your ex wasn't in it. There was a time when you were happy without her or when you thought that you'd never find someone or attract someone like her.

But you *did* find her, you did attract her, and you did love each other. She chose you over the other men pursuing her. You did have great sex together, and you did share the deepest and most intimate part of your lives together. You did share great moments and unforgettable experiences together that added to your story of life, and you did learn great lessons from each other.

What more could you want from someone? Is this not enough? Is anything missing?

You attracted someone and you both fell in love, and you can do it again. Knowing the lessons, you know now, you'll be able to do it with much greater conviction and not make the same mistakes.

But ultimately, you need to ask yourself, "Do I want her back because she met my needs in an irreplaceable way? Or because I want to escape from the pain and avoid the journey of finding a better, more suitable partner?"

The truth often hurts but leads us down the correct path in the long term.

BIG IDEAS:

1. **To fully heal from your breakup, you must understand the value she provided or didn't provide in the relationship.**
   Even if your ex broke up with *you*, there were likely parts of the relationship that didn't serve you. Apply the "Attraction Equation" and understand the value she provided versus the value she took.

2. **Understanding the "Three Whys" will give you the clarity you need to rewrite the story of your breakup.**
   Why did you start dating your ex? Why did you stay with her? Why would you want her back? When you dig deeper into these questions, it forces you out of an emotionally reactive state and challenges you to discover the truth.

3. **Accept the truth about your breakup.**
   You didn't lose the only woman who will ever love you. If you knew you couldn't fail and that six months from today you'd wake up next to a higher quality partner, would you still want your ex? Or would you want someone who is more aligned with your values and vision?

CHAPTER 6:

TRANSFORM-ING PAIN INTO GROWTH

As you regain your sense of power and confidence after a breakup, it's easy to point fingers and blame your ex for all the problems in the relationship. You not only knock her off the pedestal you'd put her on, you also bury her under a pile of anger and resentment for all the ways she caused pain, suffering, and emotional trauma.

But the truth is, you were *both* responsible for the outcome of your relationship—and the pain you experienced during it. Even if she was toxic, overly dramatic, and incompatible with you, *you* still ignored the red flags and stayed with her.

I'm not saying this to burden you with guilt or blame. Like most men, you were doing the best you could with what you knew at the time. But until you take responsibility for the failures and mistakes in the relationship, you can't learn from them. If you don't learn from the mistakes, you'll continue to repeat them in new relationships, guaranteed, so we must grow from them.

This challenge brings a potential source of life changing growth. The end of a relationship is the opportunity to discover where you went wrong and how you can improve. If you humble yourself and learn from the mistakes that led to your breakup, you can permanently level up.

These lessons will equip you to either re-enter a new relationship with your ex from a place of understanding—knowing exactly what went wrong and how you can improve—or to carry those lessons to a new relationship without repeating the same negative patterns.

Either way, you win. Whether you get back with your ex or not, this process of reflecting on and applying the lessons learned from your last relationship will give you invaluable insights that can improve your romantic life forever.

HALF-ASSED LOVERS

When my ex left, I was as confused as I was devastated. I knew that we had problems. I knew that I wasn't showing up as fully as I could. But I didn't expect her to leave so abruptly and become so cold and distant overnight, as if I meant nothing to her. I offered so much throughout our relationship and provided a level of value I knew she hadn't experienced before—yet it still wasn't enough, which hurt.

As I sat with the heartbreak, mulling over her decision and trying to make sense of what happened, I had an epiphany. It flipped everything I thought I knew about "being the man" in a relationship on its head.

You can be a high-value man, but a low-value lover.

As men, we're often conditioned to believe that our external value in society—professional success, physical attractiveness, material possessions —are sufficient to keep a woman happy. In fact, one of the most common gripes I hear from coaching clients going through a breakup or divorce is, "I gave her everything she could have ever wanted, and she still freaking left."

What they're really saying is, "I provided all of the *external* value that we're told women want in society."

But this says nothing about the quality of the internal value provided, like their level of intimacy, the emotional connection, or how they showed up for their ex's needs during that relationship. External value is necessary to create interest and spark attraction, but it isn't sufficient to make a relationship thrive in the long term.

Just look at Bill Gates, Jeff Bezos, and Elon Musk. At one point in time, they've each held the title of "World's Richest Man," yet each of them went through painful, expensive divorces. The material value they provided was insufficient to keep their partners happy in the long term, and they failed to show up with the immaterial value money can't buy—presence, connection, intimacy, positive emotions, faithfulness, and meeting core needs.

They were half-assed lovers. And after my breakup, I realized I'd fallen into a similar trap.

I provided a great quality of life for my ex on an external level. I was successful, in great shape, and maintained physically attractive as best I could. I plugged her into a fun social circle and took her on adventures and experiences she'd never had before. Throughout the relationship, I helped alleviate her stress by buying anything she needed and solving any problem she needed support with.

But I failed to consistently show up where it mattered most—in my role as her intimate lover. I'm not just talking about sex or going out, but the deeper connection she craved, to be seen, understood, and truly accepted and loved for who she was. This type of connection is rare, whereas the external value I provided is more available.

Once the "I love yous" became commonplace, I unconsciously took that as a sign that I must be doing enough in the relationship. If she is going to say this romantic phrase that we associate with the highest level of connection and intimacy in society, then I must be a great boyfriend so there is no need to invest even more of myself in the relationship. I coasted on my external value without accepting the responsibility of providing the deeper inner value, the kind that would bring us closer together, not just as partners logistically but as intimate lovers.

Ultimately, this complacency caused her to feel unloved and disconnected. It drove her to end the relationship as she felt that other men would be able to better meet her deeper internal needs.

As I reflected on that relationship—and even went so far as to reach out to previous exes for feedback—I realized that showing up fully as a lover is much simpler and less time consuming than most men believe. It isn't *easy* because it requires courage, vulnerability, and humility. But it isn't rocket science, either.

Specifically, there are key areas where men fail as lovers and several major problems which cause the most conflict in relationships. Chances are, no matter how well you think you showed up in your relationship, your ignorance about these areas may have contributed to the disconnection in your relationship.

THE SECRET PASSWORD TO HER HEART

Every woman has a different "password" to her heart. It's a specific code that will trigger her to feel desire, connection, and love. If ignored, will cause her to disconnect, be frustrated, and fall out of love.

There are a number of needs humans have, but we'll focus on five common human needs:

1. **Certainty**: to feel confident in your ability to take her and the relationship on a journey worth experiencing. She needs to know that you can handle adversity, risk and show up both financially and emotionally.

2. **Uncertainty**: creating spontaneity, adventure, and a sense of novelty. Life can't become one boring Groundhog Day of the same date nights, conversations and tv binges.

3. **Significance**: to feel important, special, seen, and needed. She needs to know that she matters to you, while also knowing that your mission and purpose in life still matter to you.

4. **Connection and Love:** to experience deep acceptance, sexual connection, emotional validation, a strong understanding of who you are and how you operate, the knowledge that you

have a strong understanding of her inner world, and to feel safe enough to be her true self without fearing judgment or from you.

5. **Growth**: a shared vision that you both agree on, support in her professional or personal goals, and the feeling that you are her ally with her goals and support her in being her best self.

The hierarchy of those needs and the unique ways in which they want those needs met varies from person to person. Without thinking too hard about it, can you identify your ex's core needs and list the specific ways she wanted those needs met? If not, then it's likely that the dysfunction in your relationship stemmed from not knowing what her needs were and how to best meet them.

Even though two women may value the same thing, the specific *way* this value manifests itself in their lives and relationships may differ.

For example, a woman who grew up in a sexually suppressed environment where money was a chronic source of stress and anxiety may have a high need for financial certainty, but an equally high need for sexual uncertainty. Or, if a woman grew up with a successful but absentee father, she may feel a higher need for connection and validation than she does for professional growth.

This is where men often encounter trouble. In most relationships, men are completely oblivious to their partner's needs and even more oblivious to the specific actions that make their partner feel as if those needs are being successfully met.

The challenge for most men is twofold. First, in the early stages of dating, few men have the emotional or romantic skills to explicitly communicate their own needs and to identify their partner's basic needs. Many people enter relationships where there is a fundamental misalignment between their needs and their partner's needs, leading to a dysfunctional relationship where one or both parties' needs are not being met.

These relationships are often doomed from the start. It's not because either partner is "wrong," but because, on a fundamental level, they both need different things. These things are never communicated so they're unable to be met. Regardless of the increasing external value the man provides, it means little until this is resolved.

Without a clear understanding of what your partner's needs are and how they expect those needs to be met, the relationship will always be plagued by a feeling like "something is off."

Even if you feel like you're doing everything right, you could be missing the target entirely, creating a silent resentment that can lead to random arguments and further disconnection.

With this foundational understanding, let's reflect on these critical questions:

1. Did you know your partner's crucial needs and the way she expected them to be met?
2. Did your partner know *your* key needs and the unique ways that you wanted those needs met? Did you fail to communicate your needs and allow your lack of communication to breed resentment?
3. Did you and your partner regularly discuss both of your needs, how they were evolving over time, and praise one another for the way you were meeting each other's needs? Did you make explicit requests for how your needs could be better met?

As in everything else, the details matter. Even though it might not seem like much, sometimes a simple monthly check-in conversation over dinner and wine about what you need, how you need it, and showing gratitude when they did meet your needs is enough to bridge a gap in communication that could have otherwise ended a relationship.

THE LANGUAGES OF LOVE

In the same way that we all have unique needs in life and from our partners, we also have unique ways of expressing and receiving love. I recommend you read, *The Five Love Languages* by author Gary Chapman, where he identified five primary ways that we give and receive love in a relationship. Here's a quick breakdown of each.

1. **Quality Time:** sharing experiences, having deep conversations, and spending focused time together
2. **Physical Affection**: displays of affection, kissing, caressing, dominant behavior, sexual needs
3. **Words of Affirmation:** verbally validating your partner, saying, "I love you," "I understand you," "I accept you," sending love texts, notes, etc
4. **Acts of Service:** doing chores or other activities to make your partner's life less stressful (like bringing her coffee in bed, cleaning up, fixing her car)
5. **Gift Giving:** knowing what she values and giving those things to her big or small. It's not the item that has value it's that know what she wants which suggests you know and listen to her well

None of these are "better" or "worse" than the other. Just like our other basic needs, they're simply unique parts of ourselves that we bring into a relationship. The challenge that arises is when partners fail to communicate their love languages and how they would like them to be met.

We often believe that our partner's love language is the same as our own and that the way you give love is equally valued as much as you do. A lot of men truly love their partner but fail to express it in a way that their partner *feels*.

It's kind of like buying someone a gift because it's what *you* would want when they have no interest in the gift. The problem isn't that they're mean or insensitive. The problem is that you failed to understand (or even to care) what they truly wanted and projected your own love language onto them, expecting them to value it the same way. It's like a guy buying his lover a new home theatre audio system when she doesn't even watch movies, but the guy does.

If you express love differently than your partner receives it, it can cause your partner to feel unloved and you to feel resentful. You *feel* like you're expressing love, but because your partner speaks a different love language, they don't receive it. And it comes across as if you don't truly know her, understand her, or listen to her.

For example, if your primary love language is acts of service, you might clean the house, make her a home-cooked breakfast, and bring her a smoothie in bed to show her how much you love her. Even though she might appreciate the gesture, if her primary love language is quality time, this gesture will fall short since what she wants is for you to stay in bed with her, cuddle, and laugh under the sheets. It isn't that she doesn't appreciate the acts of service. Rather, the way she feels *most* loved is when you give her your full and undivided attention.

Inversely, if her primary love language is words of affirmation and yours is physical affection, she might have expressed her love by telling you how important you were to her and how much she loved you, but you didn't *feel* loved because what you craved was physical intimacy.

We all give and receive love in different ways. Again, it's entirely possible for two people to love each other deeply and still feel unloved because they give and receive love in different ways. If we aren't explicitly communicating our love language, validating our partner when they speak that language, informing them what we like and don't like, and intentionally practicing our partner's love language (even if it doesn't come naturally to us), we create an avoidable but potentially devastating strain on the relationship.

The questions for you to consider in this section are:

1. If I sat down with both of you right now, would you be able to clearly articulate your ex's love language and the specific ways you could make her feel loved, and vice versa?
2. Did you and your ex explicitly discuss your unique love languages and the particular actions, words, and activities that made you both feel the most loved?
3. Did you make a consistent practice of regularly expressing love to your partner in the way that she received it? Especially if her love language didn't come naturally to you?

If not, then this is a possible root cause of the dysfunction in your relationship and what led to its end. You must take this into account if you're going to repair your relationship or show up better with your next partner.

TOTAL ACCEPTANCE

After my last relationship ended, I reached out to a previous ex from many years before in order to gain a deeper understanding of the mistakes I was making in my relationships and how I could improve in the future. During our conversation, she shared something that was equally profound and heart-wrenching.

"Andrew, during our relationship, I never felt like I was good enough. You're so focused on growth, goals, and personal development that I didn't feel like I had the space to be me. I was always struggling to keep up and I felt like you were loving me for the person I could be, not who I was."

Even though I know I'm a growth-driven person, I never realized the impact that my goals had on my lovers. I mistakenly thought that my high drive and ambition had no downsides and it was only seen as attractive and "high value".

The truth is, I loved my partners for who they were. Yes, I wanted the best for them and when they shared a goal or a problem, I supported them and stood up for their innate potential. Yet this stance came from a genuine desire to support them in getting everything they wanted out of life, *not* so I could change them into the type of woman I could love one day.

Years ago, I didn't fully grasp the lessons I've shared in the previous sections, so the way my partners received my attempts at supporting and uplifting them was wildly different from what I intended. Regardless of my positive intentions, *two* of my exes expressed feelings that I thought they weren't good enough. I made them feel like I didn't love and accept them for who they were in the present, like they needed to change and "keep up" if they were going to be a part of my growth-driven life.

Eventually, my expectations for them became too great, and they sought men who didn't make them feel inferior. They desired men who accepted them for who they were "as is," even if it meant those men might have a lower capacity to provide and were less attractive.

Yet, in their eyes, they weren't trading down—they were going after men who met their needs, which is all they wanted.

This problem is far more common than most men realize. Whether they're conscious of it or not, some men enter relationships with a desire to change or fix their lovers. They view it as a challenge or project because it makes them feel valued in the relationship. The belief is that "if I improve her life, then she must value and love me even more because I helped her." Yet, underneath this is a script that says, "Until *she* changes, I can't fully love her so I'll hold back." As a result, their partner never feels fully loved or accepted for who she is, causing disconnection and resentment. They're constantly striving to become someone they may or may not want to be in hopes that they'll be "enough" for their man.

When you think back on your relationship, ask yourself, "Did I love my partner fully for who she was? Or was my love conditional on who I wanted her to become?" If she'd stayed *exactly* the same as she was during your relationship, would you still love her in five or ten years? Or would you have left the relationship because she wasn't "enough" for you?

One of the greatest paradoxes of relationships is that the best way to support your partner's growth is to love them fully for who they are right now with no expectations about who they might become. They'll feel a deep sense of safety in the relationship, which may create an environment where she wants to change and grow on her own. They'll know that whether they succeed or fail, you'll still be there, loving them for who they are, as is, not who they might become.

RADICAL COMMUNICATION

Most couples *think* they communicate, but most couples don't communicate truthfully as much as they say what needs to be said to avoid conflict. But no matter how many "talks" they have, they rarely resolve the issue, so it just builds up until the next "talk" which is a repeat of the last but with more ferocity. The trap most couples fall into is either that they fail to communicate with any consistent cadence or, when they do communicate, they don't create a safe container where each partner feels like they're able to share their truth without fear, judgment, or ridicule.

Ask yourself: "Did my ex and I consistently set aside time alone together to share what we were feeling and experiencing, and did we check in on how the relationship was going for each other?"

For example, toward the end of one relationship, I fell into the trap of "assuming" that my partner understood why I was working so hard and so many hours. My business was going through a difficult transition and there were multiple challenges that had my stress and anxiety at an all-time high. Yet, instead of communicating this to my partner and being honest—admitting that I was scared, that I was stressed, and that I didn't have it all figured out as the man—I hid behind the alibi of being busy and pretending like everything was fine. I wanted her to see me as someone who was always doing well and not struggling.

Even though my reasons for prioritizing work were legitimate, she experienced my prioritization as neglect. She didn't understand what was happening in my world or why I was working so hard. She felt like I cared more about my work than her needs and the relationship, which led her to go out with other people in her free time since I was unavailable physically and emotionally.

If I'd had the foresight to have a regular fun date night with her and where we communicated what was really going on in our lives—being vulnerable about the challenges—she would have understood what was going on and had the option to be supportive. In fact, supporting me through the professional struggles could have been an opportunity to bring us closer together.

The second area where many men fail at the art of communication is in creating a container of safety where they and their partner can communicate honestly without fear of heavy confrontation. It doesn't matter how many times you sit down to talk with your partner or how many "important" conversations you have. Yes, you are communicating, but if you're belittling your partner's views, arguing against her feelings, and making her feel wrong for her experience and values, she won't feel safe enough to tell you the truth again. Over time, this will keep her from sharing anything important (like things that are making her unhappy or what she needs more of), which leads to resentment, disconnection, and an inevitable breakup.

For example, she might have expressed how she was feeling disconnected from you because you weren't spending enough quality time together. In this situation, most men will lash out and exclaim, "Are you serious? We went on a date last week and I spent so much money! Why are you so needy?"

Not only does this reactive response focus only on external value and display an inability to stay grounded, it severs emotional connection and teaches your partner that you aren't "safe" to open up to. She can't fully express herself to you without judgment or reprisal. So why even bother? It teaches her to be silent about the very things that could bring you closer together, things that would prevent dysfunction from manifesting.

Finally, and perhaps the most challenging component of effective communication for men, is the concept of validation. When most men experience an unpleasant emotion or sensation, their gut instinct is to immediately try to fix it or find a logical explanation for why it's happening. Women, on the other hand, work through their emotions by expressing them.

A friend of mine shared an example that perfectly encapsulated this point. He and his wife were going out with friends and, as they were getting ready, his wife began complaining about her appearance. She felt bloated and unattractive in her outfit. And in response, he invalidated her insecurity, even though he thought he was helping.

"Are you kidding me?" he exclaimed, "You've got to stop being so insecure! Seriously, you look good. Have some confidence in yourself. I know a good book for you to read."

On the surface, this response might not look that bad. But it led to a thirty-minute argument that almost ruined their night out. Then, the next day, as they were getting ready to go swimming with another couple, the other woman expressed the same emotion. She hated the way her swimsuit made her feel and was on the verge of tears because of how she felt about herself.

But her husband's response was wildly different from my friend's. He hugged his wife and told her, "I'm so sorry you feel that way. I know it sucks when you don't feel like yourself—especially in a swimsuit—but I just want you to know I think you look insanely hot."

The difference between these two responses is that in the second one, he validated and empathized with his wife's emotions before attempting to uplift her and shift her into a more positive state. My friend, on the other hand, invalidated his wife's experience and made her feel "wrong" for feeling bad about herself (in other words, he made her feel bad about feeling bad) and shifted her into a negative state.

This principle applies across a plethora of issues. In my relationship, my partner would regularly complain about challenges at work or issues with her co-workers, and my gut instinct was to tell her why she should change her mindset and how to solve the issue with clear action steps.

Every time I did this, it drove a wider wedge between us until she learned that it wasn't safe to share her emotions with me, not just with work but also about our relationship. If I'd instead validated her experience and made her feel justified *before* sharing a direct solution, her response would have been wildly different. If a woman does not feel heard and seen first, she will not be open to any solution you offer. She will keep repeating herself in different ways until you do.

Think back on the ways you communicated in your relationship and consider the following questions:

- Did I regularly make time and emotional space to communicate with my ex where we were both fully present and engaged?
- Did I listen and validate her emotional experience before sharing my reflections and disagreements? Or did I make her feel "wrong" for her emotions and attempt to show her why she shouldn't feel the way she did?
- Did I communicate in a way that made my partner feel heard, understood, and safe? Or did I communicate defensively? Did I come across like she was the opposing legal team in a heated courtroom battle and I desperately needed to be right out of ego?

- Did I fully communicate my own experience and take ownership over that experience—the difference between, "You made me feel bad" and "When you said this, I felt this way"—or did I avoid vulnerability and displays of emotion to show that I was "strong?"
- Did you always have to be right?

THE SLOW DEATH OF COMPLACENCY

In relationships and in life, last month's performance isn't enough to win today's game. It doesn't matter how great things were when the relationship started, what matters is how you're showing up *right now*. It matters very little how many date nights, vacations or wild romantic experiences you shared in the past, what matters is how you're connecting yesterday and today.

And of all the ways that men unwittingly sabotage their relationships, complacency is the most common and silent.

In the early stages of a romance, it's easy to show up fully, to be present, to communicate. The connection is new and exciting, and you haven't been together long enough for the problems and mismatch to start. All the dopamine and oxytocin in the brain is firing on all cylinders making you miss and love each other. But as time wears on and the chemicals are reduced, it becomes easy to take your partner for granted.

Once we regularly hear our partner say, "I love you," we believe that we've "won" and so we stop putting in additional effort. We then shift our focus on other areas of life. Sometimes, it's normal to prioritize your career or health or family more than your relationship for some time. But when this goes on for too long and there's no communication, disconnection, and resentment can foster. Regardless of the other goals or challenges in your life, you *must* show up in the present consistently to make a relationship work in the long run… period.

All too often we rely on the good times of the past to carry the relationship forward, instead of actively creating new experiences and a stronger connection today. As you know, falling in love is not a guarantee of *staying* in love. And this is a lesson many men have to learn the hard way.

Just like you can't expect last year's workouts to keep you in great shape or rely on last year's award at work to carry your career, you can't rely on the love and positive experiences you shared six months ago or even six weeks ago to be sufficient to grow the relationship *today*. For instance, if a player wins MVP years ago but then fails to keep that level of dedication and commitment to the sport in the present, when they stop performing and showing up, their team may trade them out for a player who's showing up better *today* or reduce his pay.

The same is true in relationships. When you stop showing up, providing value, and meeting her needs, she's either going to scout for a better "player" or reduce the "contract." In other words, she will find a new partner or reduce the value she offers in the relationship (less connection, kind gestures, meeting your sexual needs).

Although it's painful to admit, the reason your relationship might have ended was because you simply stopped caring about the relationship as much as you used to. You stopped putting in the effort and doing the things that allowed her to fall in love with you in the first place. When you look at the last few months preceding your breakup, how were you showing up?

- Did you become complacent from hearing "I love you" so much that it made you feel like there's no point in showing up more than you already are?
- Were you intentionally creating time for emotional connection and intimacy?
- Did you have a consistent cadence of connection like weekly date nights, monthly experiences, mini or big vacations, or did you haphazardly prioritize your relationship only when it was in trouble?

To fully capture the lessons from your breakup, you need to not only understand *where* you went wrong, but *why* this happened. The "why" will reveal even deeper lessons you need to uncover.

- Did you stop caring because you chose a partner who isn't compatible and decided that settling was preferable to the pain of leaving?
- Did you stop showing up because you took her for granted and assumed that the relationship had been won when she said "I love you" or moved in with you?
- Did you even realize that you'd grown complacent because your communication was shallow and infrequent?

The deeper you dig below the surface of *what* happened to understand *why* it happened, the greater your growth and future success will be.

MAKE THE STRUGGLE WORTH IT

One uncomfortable truth is that our greatest growth is often found from our greatest pain. But you must be willing to face that pain and not hide from it, or else you risk repeating the same mistakes and missing something new in front of you. You must pay attention and learn some hard lessons in order to grow stronger and become who you are meant to be.

After you sit with the lessons and questions shared in this chapter, I want you to ask yourself something that will bring everything home:

If the entire purpose of this relationship was for you to learn three critical lessons about yourself and your way of being in relationships— what would those critical lessons be? And would they make all of this pain worth it?

You can choose lessons you've identified from previous sections or new ones that you've uncovered based on what you are learning. You'll likely come up with new lessons overtime as these concepts sink in. It will help you reflect and say, "I needed that experience in order to get to where I am today," and do it with a smile.

There are probably dozens of lessons you can take from your separation. But there are only a small handful that—if applied consistently—will fundamentally alter who you are and how you show up to relationships in the future. The challenge is to find the most crucial ones and never forget them. Make them your rules for a successful relationship moving forward.

You've earned them.

BIG IDEAS:

1. **You either learn from your mistakes or repeat them.**
   Moments of pain are opportunities for growth, but you must be willing to humble yourself and *learn* from the mistakes that caused the pain. If you don't learn from the mistakes that caused your relationship to end (including the mistakes you made during the *selection* process of your relationship), you'll repeat those mistakes in the future and experience the same pain you're experiencing now.

2. **You can be a high-value man, but a low-value lover.**
   It doesn't matter how much money you make, how big your biceps are, or how much material resources you offer, if you aren't showing up for your partner in the way *she* needs—knowing her needs, speaking her love language, and accepting her fully—you are offering little value as a lover which will inevitably end the relationship regardless of the material value provided.

3. **The greatest killer of relationships is complacency.**
   Nothing will kill a relationship faster than believing that you've "won." It matters little if your partner says, "I love you," frequently… or even "I do." Yesterday's victories aren't worth a damn *today*. The way to maintain a successful relationship over time is to continually show up and prioritize the relationship today. Complacency paves the road to ruin in all aspects of life.

CHAPTER 7:

DANCING WITH FIRE

Three months after my breakup, I started to notice something interesting. Even though my life was moving forward at full speed and the power of the core commitments had accelerated every life journey I was on, something still felt a little "off." Anytime I was with a new woman, I felt blocked emotionally, intimately, and even sexually, like there was an invisible force holding me in place and preventing me from moving forward with them.

At first, I tried to shrug it off, thinking, "This will pass with time." But as time went on, nothing seemed to change and the more I sat with it, the more I realized an "inconvenient" truth—I still had unresolved feelings for my ex.

Let me be clear. By this point, I'd reclaimed my power that I'd lost at the onset of the breakup. The pedestal I'd placed my ex on during the early days of the breakup had been knocked down. I no longer *needed* her in order to feel healthy, happy, or whole.

But I still had an emotional attachment to her because I had loved her dearly for some time. I wanted to touch base and see where we are both at.

The problem was, we hadn't spoken in nearly three and a half months. I had no idea what was going on in her life, what she was feeling, how she was doing, or if she was dating someone new. I was curious about where she was on her journey.

- Had her feelings changed?
- Did she miss having me in her life?
- Did she think I was angry with her and felt scared to reach out?
- Was she happy with the breakup and not looking back?

I couldn't help but wonder, "What if?" What if all of the pain we'd experienced together was exactly what we needed in order to learn key lessons for a new relationship to succeed? What if she'd grown and we were now a better fit for each other's lives? Or, what if nothing had changed, and I was better off letting her go and moving on with my life?

And so, after several conversations with close friends, I decided it was time to reach out and break "no contact".

REQUIREMENTS FOR REACHING OUT

In a perfect world, you won't have to consider whether or not you're ready to reach out to her because she'll make the first move (or you'll decide that you don't have any future interest in her after the lessons learned in previous chapters). However, there are requirements that *must* be met before you can reach out to her.

1. Time and Space

Enough time has passed for both of you to fully experience the reality of being separated and to reflect on the relationship and the lessons learned from it. However, "enough time" will look different for every man.

As a general rule, 10 to 16 weeks is a healthy minimum for *most* situations. It gives you enough time to experience the benefits of the core commitments. It gives both of you enough time to experience what life is like without each other and if you want that reality. It gives time for possible dating and lets you both discover if this is something you like or don't like. It gives both of you the time and space you need for your heavy emotions to settle and the truth to emerge.

But ultimately, this is a decision that will be made at your discretion. If you're considering reaching out but feel unsure, I encourage you to wait and discuss the decision with friends or mentors before taking action. You must not act from a place of emotional reaction and heightened anxiety based on what she's doing, which can worsen the situation.

Remember, you can always reach out *later*. Tomorrow, next week, or next month. But once you break "no contact," there's no going back. If you don't feel ready, then don't do it.

2. Progress on the Core Commitments

You have shown up to the core commitments in chapter 4 to increase your value and decrease neediness as best you can. Without the increased sense of confidence, self-esteem, and worth that comes from these commitments, you probably won't have identified critical lessons about the breakup. You also probably won't be in a healthy emotional and psychological state that lets you have a positive interaction with your ex.

3. Positive Interactions with Quality Women

Although you don't need to sleep with new women during your initial separation from your ex, it's important that you're having positive social interactions with women that you're attracted to. You need to see with your own eyes that your ex isn't the only woman you can experience positive emotions, connection, and fun with.

Ideally, having casual dates or being social and flirtatious in group settings helps build an abundance mentality and shifts you out of scarcity. If you don't *feel* abundant and know in your bones that you're a high-value man, it will show and be felt. Your body language, vocal tonality, and communication will ooze with desperation, and she'll smell it like a shark smells blood.

Although this requirement is difficult to quantify objectively, you can ask yourself a simple question to determine whether or not you're ready to reach out: "Do I believe there are other women I could create a better connection with than my ex?" If the answer is "no", then you aren't ready.

4. A Deep Sense of Clarity

Let's assume you've done the exercises in chapters five and six and reached a point of deep clarity with yourself about your relationship. If I met you on the street and asked you to tell me the specific value that your ex provided, the value she required from you in return, and the most important lessons you learned from your relationship, you should be able to answer without hesitation, telling me clearly and without stumbling over your words and thinking too long about it.

Until you've removed her from the pedestal—and realized that she isn't a goddess who can do no wrong—you aren't ready to reach out. Until you understand what went wrong both in your own life and in the relationship, you'll have no understanding of what you can improve or what you need to avoid if the two of you *do* get back together. Even if she takes you back with open arms, the relationship will be a ticking time bomb, waiting for the same conflicts to set off the fuse and cause an explosion.

If you show up as the same man you were before and expect things to magically work out, you are guaranteeing failure. However, if you both know what went wrong, why it went wrong, and are actively taking action to improve, there is *potential* that you and your ex can work in the long term.

5. Shift from Desperation to Curiosity

When I reached out to my ex, I didn't do so from a place of weakness, neediness, or scarcity. My life was thriving without her, and I knew that I could continue living a high-quality life, whether or not I ever spoke to her again.

But I was curious about where she was on her journey and how she'd been since the breakup. I was curious if we could start talking again at a minimum, seeing where that could go and if it would supersede the other women I was talking to.

I *wanted* to contact her, but I didn't *need* to. I was curious about her, but I didn't need her in order to be happy. I was capable of moving on and thriving, regardless of her response.

This mindset is a critical prerequisite before breaking "no contact." Until you experience this shift, you aren't ready to reach out. If you believe you've met all of the requirements (and people closest to you support your decision) you are now in a position where you can reach out.

HOW TO REACH OUT AND RECONNECT

To successfully reconnect with your ex, it's important that you continue to act from the same grounded frame you've held throughout the "no contact" period. Again, in an ideal world, she will reach out to *you*, and you'll be able to spark a connection and schedule a time to meet up in person.

But there's no guarantee that will happen. What's more likely is:

1. **She will reach out indirectly (commenting, viewing, or liking a social media post or asking about you through a mutual friend).**

It's unlikely that she'll explicitly tell you that she misses you and wants to meet up. Instead, she might test the waters to see how you react. Do not treat a social media "like" or comment the same as a direct text message or phone call.

Indirect contact is often used to gauge your interest. Are you still on standby and waiting for her to reach out? Have you really changed? Or are you still the needy, angry, and hurt man she left in the first place?

Remember, every action you take moving forward needs to be filtered through the question, "What would the prize do?"

If you have *truly* regained your power, then any form of communication she makes should be interesting but not overly exciting. Instead of immediately texting, commenting back, or following her, simply acknowledge and trust that this is a good sign. She's thinking about you. She's looking at your social media. She's interested in your life and whereabouts. All of these are a precursor to attraction.

Stay calm, stay grounded, and generally ignore these indirect attempts. Stay focused on the core commitments, posting positive content on social media (without bragging or overtly showing off any women you're dating) and trusting that eventually she'll reach out directly via a text or call.

2. You reach out to her and spark a connection.
If she doesn't reach out, don't freak out. That doesn't mean that her feelings are gone or that she no longer cares about you. It's possible she doesn't want to risk rejection from you. She knows that she hurt you and she doesn't know how you're feeling right now.

In either case, your goal is to remain calm and be the high-value man.

THREE SIMPLE WAYS TO INITIATE A CONVERSATION WITH YOUR EX

If you're contemplating reaching out, there's probably a subconscious script deep in your mind causing you to believe that the *words* you use when you reach out matter. That there's a "magic seven-word text" that will make her respond instantly and fall head over heels in love with you. It's also not true that if you get it wrong, she'll never think about you again and all the hard work you did will be in vain.

As such, you'll be tempted to overanalyze every word like a mad scientist. Writing, deleting, and rewriting that first text dozens of times to get it perfect. If you are doing this, then this is a sign that you aren't ready to reach out yet and should refocus on the core commitments.

But I'm here to tell you that this first message actually matters very little. The *real* hard work is everything that we've done up until this point: the time, the space, leaving her alone, and working on yourself to become a higher-value man.

Even something as simple as, "Hey, how are you doing?" is enough to elicit a response and get a conversation started. But there are a few other ways I've used in the past that can take some of the pressure off and make it easier to send that first message.

1. The Forgotten Item
When I reached out to my ex, my reason was simple. I'd left my spare laptop at her place before we broke up, and I wanted it back since I actually needed it for work. Days following the breakup, I knew that I'd

left it at her place, but I decided not to retrieve it because I felt time and space away from each other was more important.

When I reached out, I said:

"Hey, hope you're doing well. I need to pick up my laptop at your place. It has some data on it that I need for work."

2. The New Device

Another option that works, *if this is true*, is to say:

"Hey, I got a new phone/computer and was transferring photos and came across some of us that made me think of you. How are you?"

3. Reminiscing

If you find yourself at a venue or location that the two of you would often go to together, you can reach out with a simple:

"Hey, I was at [specific memory/place] and it made me think of you. How are you?"

If you want to put your own spin on these messages, that's fine. Just keep it short, to the point, and not emotional or romantic. Remember, you aren't her lover. You're reaching out to open lines of safe communication and pull on the thread of curiosity to gather more data about her.

RULES OF COMMUNICATION

Once a connection has been established and she's responded to your message, it's important that you keep things respectful, polite, and simple. Wait fifteen to thirty minutes before responding to avoid coming off as too eager or excited. Remember, she's not on the pedestal. She's *an* option under review, not *the* only option.

When you first reconnect, you both need time and space to let the interactions sink in. She may have been thinking about you for some time too, but this is the first time the two of you have directly communicated. It's normal if she takes several hours or even days to respond, and it might be helpful to mirror the amount of time she takes to respond. If she takes an hour to respond, then take an hour and some change to respond.

Your goal isn't to have a long text conversation where you bare your emotions, ramble on about everything you've been up to in significant detail, how much you've grown and how awesome you are and tell her how much you miss her. Your goal is to establish open lines of communication that are polite, enjoyable and respectful. A short chat is okay, yet the aim is to schedule a time where you can meet up in person to connect further. You will never text your way into anything meaningful. It must be done in person. She needs to see the changes you've made and the ways you've grown with her own eyes for her feelings to change in a meaningful way.

If, after exchanging a few messages, she doesn't seem interested in meeting up or is taking several days to respond with short and cold messages, the best path forward is to back off and give her more time and space. More communication from you is not the answer. The worst thing that you can do at this point is to try and force an encounter to happen before she's ready. And honestly, you shouldn't have to.

If you've truly met all of the requirements for reaching out, then you should be in a place where you would be *disappointed* if she isn't interested, but not emotionally *devastated*.

WHAT TO DO IF SHE DOESN'T RESPOND

Take this as a sign that she isn't ready, back off, and continue thriving in life and connecting with people who want to be in your life. Do *not* make the situation worse by blowing up her phone, sending multiple unanswered messages, or reaching out on different platforms (e.g. email, social media, apps). No matter how badly you want to see and hear from her, just know that she received your message and she isn't interested right now, or she needs more time before she's ready to respond.

This doesn't mean that she won't be open to reconnecting in the future. But she isn't at the moment when you are, and that's perfectly okay. She might respond in time, but it needs to be because of her own interest, not from guilt tripping, manipulating, or pressuring her.

You must go back to not contacting her. Stay grounded. Stay focused on your core commitments and be patient. She will respond if she wants to, but only if you give her enough time and space and just let her be.

RELEASE THE FANTASY EXPECTATIONS

After contact has been reestablished, regardless of who initiates it, the actions you take before, during, and after your first interaction can make or break the future of any relationship with your ex. One of the most dangerous things you can do is to enter into the interaction with the wrong expectations. Whether you want her back or simply want to make peace and get clarity on some things to help you heal, neither of those will happen if your interactions are coming from the wrong frame.

You are no longer her boyfriend or husband. She is no longer your partner. You should not act like one and don't expect her to, either. No matter how badly you may want that position and intimate dynamic back, that isn't going to change during your first encounter.

What's more, it *shouldn't* change.

If you've done the work outlined in this book and truly met the requirements for reconnection, you should be at a point in your journey where you aren't sure if she's the right person for you anymore. You might acknowledge that you still have feelings for her because you are a healthy human who cared for her, but despite those emotions, you should also recognize that feelings alone are not enough for a successful relationship to work in the long term.

But many of you are ready because you've changed. You've grown. You've learned new lessons about yourself, about her, and about the relationship. These lessons should cast a shadow on your future together and cause you to doubt whether a new relationship with her is truly your best option moving forward.

The question you need to answer is, "Can we reinvent this relationship together in a way that meets both of our needs or not?"

It's unlikely that you can answer this question based on a single encounter. It's likely going to take more time before both of you can come to the conclusion of what you want or don't want. You wouldn't go on one date with a new woman then profess your love and ask her to marry you, and you shouldn't assume that just because you and your ex had a relationship in the past and have agreed to meetup, that a new relationship will quickly begin or is the best path to pursue.

In some rare cases, you may indeed get back together soon after the first interaction. Because of the time you spent apart and the work you did on yourselves as individuals, you'll both know that you want to try again, and it can sometimes be obvious from the first interaction. But this shouldn't be expected.

What's more likely is that it will take a series of interactions to rebuild the attraction she felt for you and vice versa. You need to remember that regardless of how quickly the two of you move forward with a new relationship, it's exactly that: a *new* relationship. Building new things takes time. It also takes commitment from *both* partners. She needs to be willing to show up and work with you on the challenges you experienced together with as much energy and enthusiasm as you have.

Understanding this, you should treat every encounter moving forward as if you're dating her again for the first time. You're learning about who she is, how she's changed, and whether or not she's a good fit for your life. Even if *she* expresses a desire to get back together, you can certainly be open to it, but don't be fully sold too quickly and too fervently.

Be curious, reserved, and careful not to rush into any new relationship with your ex. Take things slowly and one day at a time. Prioritize the core commitments as your default setting for the future over chasing your ex.

Not only is this frame important for your *own* sanity and attractiveness to her, remember, you just went through one of the most traumatic and painful experiences a human can have (the loss of a loved one) because of a decision *she* likely made. When you meet, whether she's consciously aware of it or not, she *will* be testing you and gauging your value. She wants to know whether you've really changed. She wants to know if you are still obsessing over her and have her on a pedestal. She wants to see if your value has increased or decreased, if you internalized the lessons you needed to learn, and if you're the best option now that she's had a taste of life without you.

It's more important now than ever that you maintain control of your emotions and lead in an attractive, grounded way with your power intact.

NAVIGATING THE FIRST ENCOUNTER SUCCESSFULLY

No matter how you feel right now, the moment that you make contact, especially during those first moments, your emotions will be at an all-time high. Your mind will be spiraling, your heart aching, and all of the work that you've done up until this point will be put to the test. Despite the successes I achieved and the growth I experienced during my period of "no contact," the second I saw my ex again, it was like stepping into a whirlwind of emotions, unresolved conflict and excitement all wrapped in one.

You need to prepare yourself for this. You're gearing up for an emotional fight not with *her*, but with your own emotional impulses that want answers immediately about why things happened and what went wrong.

Regardless of what form these impulses take, you will be tempted to act out of alignment with your values and the lessons in this book. You may be tempted to "fix" everything during the first interaction. Your impulse might be to overshare exactly what you've learned, where you went wrong, where she went wrong, and how you can successfully move forward. You might share how you're going to buy her all the things she shared she wanted in the past. You may be tempted to bare your soul, profess your undying love, and share every mistake you made in the past and every way you're going to improve in the future. You might freak out when she mentions another man's name whether it's a platonic or romantic relationship. You may even want to lash out in anger and tear her apart with a verbal storm of emotion for the pain she put you through.

You *will* be tempted, but just because you feel that way, that doesn't mean it will lead to the best results.

Let's start with how a high-value man *would* and *would not* act during the first few encounters. Specifically, a high-value man *would*:

- Be alive, positive, and outgoing
- Be thriving in life without her
- Be sharing adventurous stories about his life since the breakup
- Be doing well mentally, professionally, physically, and socially
- Be enjoying the interaction you're sharing together in the present moment and not living in his head
- Be open to the idea of getting back together but uncertain if it's the right decision so soon

Remember, right now you're not sure if you want her back in your life. She's an option under review. You're simply gathering more data. The experience should be fun, playful, and lighthearted. You don't know how she's changed or where she's at in her life.

Just as importantly, *she* doesn't yet know if she's interested in you. She doesn't know what you've been up to, how you've changed or how you've grown. As such, during your first interaction, she's trying to figure out whether or not you will be a friend or a possible lover. If you feel like she is trying to friendzone you, then you should confidently and calmly make it clear that you are *not* looking to be friends.

When I first met up with my ex, I could feel the interaction becoming too platonic and friendly and she was keeping her distance. I could *feel* myself getting friendzoned. And I wasn't interested in it. I firmly told her:

"You know I'll never just be your friend, right? I met you and we became lovers within minutes. That's the only way I've ever known you. We've been intimate hundreds of times and we have too much shared history to be just friends."

Not only did she accept this, but by holding my ground, she became less closed off and opened up more physically and emotionally throughout the rest of the interaction.

While there are no guarantees that your ex will respond in the same way, I encourage you to take a similar firm stance. If the two of you try to maintain a platonic relationship when you wanted to get back together with her, you're being inauthentic and settling for whatever you can get, which will only communicate low value, neediness and desperation.

Now, we also have a clear set of ground rules for what a high-value man would *not* do during the interaction. He would not:

- Beg, plead, or confess the depth of pain he experiences without her
- Try to force a new relationship to begin during the first encounter before he leaves out of fear he'll never see her again
- Manipulate or pressure her into sharing feelings she's not ready to share
- Express anger, jealousy, hostility or create conflict
- Be overly invested in getting back together so soon… or at all
- Be on standby and waiting for her to return while she continues to "explore"
- Be willing to be her "friend" in hopes that she'll fall for him later

Even if you're able to stand firm against temptation, your internal fight doesn't end once the interaction begins and you're having a good time together. If you're fun, positive, and playful and she responds *positively*, you'll be tempted to escalate the interaction and may come on too strongly, too fast, and try to force a reconciliation on the spot. If she responds *negatively*, you may react with neediness, anger or an emotional outburst in order to regain control, only making the situation worse.

Either path leads to failure.

The key to a successful interaction is to control your own frame and focus on reconnecting, learning more about her experience, and *showing*—not telling—her that you've improved and grown in the time that you've been a part.

This doesn't mean you should overtly brag about how well you're doing without her or parade around the other women you've been dating to make her jealous. It doesn't mean that you can't be vulnerable and have heartfelt conversations about the times you shared together or your thoughts on spending more time together.

Rather, lead the interaction with a fun, playful, and positive frame initially and let the rest of the interaction unfold organically. Again, if you were dating her for the first time, how would you act? How would you show up? What would you say? Lean into that.

If she opens up conversations about the past relationship or is genuinely curious about your dating life or experiences since the breakup, that's okay since it's organically happening. Topics should arise naturally, rather than through force or egoic bragging. Preferably she'll bring up these topics first, which shows she has a genuine interest and will listen.

Once your time together ends, it's important that you continue to maintain an attractive, high-value frame. Just because you've broken "no contact," spoken to her, and may have had a good interaction, it doesn't mean that you're free to call, text, or show up at her place as if you are suddenly back in a relationship. You must continue acting as if you've just met, as if you were dating someone new. Take things slow. Allow her time and space to be drawn back to you.

However, if *she* is clear that she doesn't want any future relationship with you or she is hostile and disrespectful, then walk away. Do not beg, profess your love, or cry to make her feel sorry for you in the hopes of changing her mind. No amount of logic or manipulation is going to change the situation *right now*. Confidently and gracefully wish her well, then leave with your dignity intact. No hostile last words, door slamming, throwing items, or emotional outburst of any sort is necessary.

Depending on the cause and intensity of your breakup, she may still carry unresolved resentment, trauma, or anger—and that's fine. This doesn't necessarily mean that she doesn't care about you or even that you'll never get back together in the future. It means that she isn't in a place to have a productive and healthy conversation with you *right now*.

Instead of fighting fire with fire or reacting emotionally from a weak frame, get up and calmly leave. That will speak volumes to her about what you will and will not allow, and it's the most attractive thing you can do in that moment.

SHOULD YOU HAVE SEX?

If the interaction goes *very* well, it's possible that there will be an opportunity to have sex. We must remember that you don't have enough information after *one* interaction to know whether or not the two of you should get back together. You shouldn't feel certain that she's a good fit for your life *yet*.

Sex may complicate your feelings and cloud your judgement. Sex releases a cocktail of "feel good" hormones and chemicals that can override logic and reason. It makes it all too easy to justify acting *against* your values and undoing the life changing work you did in this book. After sex, your intense desire for her may breed neediness, clinginess, and make you jealous if she's talking to other men, which she likely is at some level.

Even though it's probably one of the things you've been craving *most* since your breakup, I encourage you to delay gratification and wait until your second or third encounter before sex. That way, you can think clearly about what you're doing. Making her wait and creating a buildup of positive emotions is the better route for long-term success anyways.

Yes, there are obvious benefits to having sex on the first encounter— namely that it ensures you stay out of the friend zone, rekindles old feelings, and brings you closer together in that moment. She'll experience the same positive hormones and chemicals that *you* experience, but that can either make her more likely to want to see you again *or* create intense feelings of confusion and regret, as if it happened too fast and was a mistake, especially if alcohol was involved.

However, if you aren't feeling fully grounded during the interaction, sex can make it harder to continue acting like a high-value man. You'll feel tempted to pursue her more aggressively than you should and try to move forward too quickly. It's important to keep in mind that having sex doesn't mean you're back together. It simply means you had sex and still need to figure things out. I've heard many stories from clients where two former exes rekindled and had sex on the first encounter, only to have her ghost the man and be uninterested soon after. Perhaps being too easily won over and sexually available so soon shows that you are not the prize.

Ultimately, the choice is yours. There are pros and cons to sex with an ex. But just remember, you have little to lose by taking things slow, delaying gratification, and allowing her to chase you. So, you either realize she *is* a good option, you *do* want her back, and later you have the most mind-blowing sex together, or you decide with a clear head that she isn't the right fit for you and confidently move on.

REBUILD OR RELINQUISH

After I met up with my ex again for the first time, I was on cloud nine. The time we shared together went better than I could have imagined, and we shared some passionate kissing. But in the days that followed, I began to reflect on the interaction through the lens of my values and the lessons I'd discovered throughout my breakup journey.

I have zero animosity toward her, I will always care for her, and I want nothing but the best for her and her future. Yet, I couldn't deny that when I looked at *her* actions and my actions post breakup, they were wildly different.

She had lost her job weeks before we broke up and I was curious to see what she was doing for work, but discovered she was still unemployed and hadn't made much progress. Instead of using the time we spent apart to grow, introspect, and develop her career (I'm sure she did some of this, but her actions tell a story), she was caught up in the party scene. It seemed like every weekend was a bender of drugs, alcohol, and staying up late.

Most of our conversations during that interaction centered around all the fun she was having, and not much about growth, goals, or what she's going to do in her future when asked. It seemed like she was living for the nights and masking her life situation by partying, meeting new people and endless entertainment.

I enjoy the occasional show, festival, or fun night out, but that isn't what my life is built on. During this season of my life, I want to live more intentionally. I value waking up early, doing meaningful work, building my career, dating intentionally, being healthy and fit, and going on hikes, surfing, and having deep conversations with the people I love. I want peace.

Even when confronted with the objective facts that we were on different paths in life, and despite that I was dating other quality women who *were* aligned with my views on life, my brain still rebelled when I saw her again. My emotions went into hyperdrive and I ignored the red flags.

She is an attractive woman. I always liked her energy and provocative vibe when spending time with her. My heart (okay, and my penis) wanted to be with her, to play, to laugh, to have fun, to have sex, to go on adventures, to grow with her... but my logical mind was sounding the alarm.

The more I journaled, the more I realized her seductive nature blinded me during the entire relationship. It masked the fact that we are two different people with different values and visions for life. She was my cocaine, and I was addicted to her.

I craved the way she made me feel and the "high" I got from spending time with her. Like all addictions, she overrode my rational thoughts and drove me to act against who I was and what I valued. The comedown of not being with her was agonizing and the only way to cure it was to go back for more, but for how long and at what cost?

I was experiencing post-breakup withdrawals where I just wanted her back, regardless of the warning bells. Beyond the spell she had cast on me, my ego wanted me to get back with her simply to prove that I could. But I couldn't help but wonder, if I won that game, was it a winning relationship?

I had to get real and ask myself tough questions. Would this woman drain me or fuel me moving forward? Would she be a value-add to my vision and the life I want or a barrier to it? Does she support me in becoming the best version of myself personally and professionally? In her current state today, if she were to get pregnant, would she be a great mother and partner to raise kids with or does that picture create abject terror?

I really *loved* her (or was *addicted* to her), but that encounter together gave me further confirmation that we were on different paths in life and I couldn't ignore this.

I want to be clear. I'm not here to tell you what to do, but your gut is likely telling you what to do. However, if you truly believe that you *should* get back together, then I will share how you can do that later. But be wary of making this decision based on your emotions, ego, or worse, your penis. Your emotions and biology don't care about your best interests over the long term. They care about avoiding pain and reproducing in the short term, even if that comes with the cost of long-term consequences.

> **Ultimately, the defining moment in every man's life will be when he is forced to choose between what is uncomfortably *right* and what is comfortably *easy*.**

And the more I played the story forward and considered what my future would look like if I continued to pursue my ex—compared to a future with a more aligned woman who was in a more aligned season of life—the decision was obvious. The comfort of the familiar wasn't worth the inevitable consequences.

It is very likely that I would have found myself in the exact place you're in now, having to endure another gut-wrenching breakup, having to go through the emotional chaos again, extending my recovery process and making me emotionally unavailable to new women who could be a better fit.

You must consider the opportunity cost of going back to an ex and risking the time that could be spent fully recovering, improving your life, and attracting a new, more aligned partner. It's a massive risk, and since we're only getting older with each passing year, we must think long term… not what is comfortable and feels good today. And damnit I know it's hard to do!

After you meet up with your ex and gather the data you need (which may take several interactions), think deeply about the type of life you want to create. Is she the right person for that? Do you want to get back together to escape the pain you're feeling right now? Or because there's real compatibility and the potential for a life-giving relationship that improves both of your lives?

You're in a phase of deep introspection, so pay close attention to her *actions* and ignore her *words*. The way that she's acted since the breakup is who she *really* is and the direction she's headed, and she's unlikely to change just for you. If she's been acting in a way that conflicts with your values and the vision you have for your future, she'll continue acting that way regardless of how much she says she loves you.

She may tell you about all the things she's *going* to do or share stories about what she *wants* in the future. But if these words and stories consistently clash with what she's doing in reality, bet on the actions, not the words.

Give yourself the gift of time, space, and solitude. What would your future self in ten years tell you to do right now? If you have or had a son, and he was in your shoes, what would you tell your son to do? Are you feeling a "hell yes" about her? If not, it's simply a "hell no." There is no middle ground when it comes to going back to an ex. The stakes are too high.

Take at least a week where your contact with your ex is minimal. Go for long walks, hikes, journal, meditate and contemplate about the decision in front of you. Do not consult with her friends or family, only speak with the most trusted people in your life.

If you defy your values to appease your emotional state, ego, or sex drive, the pain will only be worse in the long run. Whether it's another heart-wrenching breakup months or years down the line, or worse, building a *family* with a person who does not share your same values and vision, you *will* be forced to pay the heavy price tomorrow for choosing comfort today. Don't be afraid to start anew because you're not starting from zero, you're starting with immense experience and lessons learned that will make any future relationship better.

REKINDLING INTIMACY AND CONNECTION

If, after thinking through the decision fully and feeling confident that you are acting from a place of values not emotion, vision not ego, abundance not sex, you may firmly decide to pursue a new relationship with your ex. The way you navigate the next encounters of the process are pivotal. As you go through these encounters, it's important to keep the "Attraction Equation" at the forefront of your mind. Remember,

Attraction = Value - Neediness

Are you adding value or taking value? Because of the history that you've shared together, this equation is working both for you and against you. You have *more* value than the other men she's considering because you have a shared history of positive experiences together. You've been intimate many times and you already have a pre-existing connection with her, her friends, and family that would take many months, if not years, to replicate with a new partner.

But as a part of that shared history, she's also seen the unattractive side of you. She's fallen in love with you *and* fallen out of love with you. It will take time for her to be convinced that you've changed and that this "new you" before her is actually the man who will be showing up to a future relationship. Her guard is up and she's still not certain that this isn't all a ruse.

As such, it will take time and patience for the two of you to rebuild connection, intimacy, and trust. You cannot rush or force this process through logical manipulation or "mansplaining" why you're perfect for her. It's not as simple as picking up where you left off before the breakup. The relationship isn't where it was before because it's been destroyed. It needs time and effort from both of you to start something new.

This is why you have to show her with your *actions*, not your words, that you have changed, that your value has increased, and that the man she broke up with has grown into a better lover.

You must maintain the frame that you *want* her, but you don't *need* her. Take things slowly, allowing her to come back to you naturally rather than through high-pressure conversations. Remember, even if the two of you never get back together, you've still won. You've grown, you've learned, and you're on the path to a bigger and brighter future—with or without her.

But what if you *need* her back? Then the odds are high that you'll do something pathetic to humiliate yourself and make the situation worse.

Again, I encourage you to treat the early encounters with your ex as if you're dating her for the first time. Even if you had an amazing first interaction—and even if you were intimate—you are *not* fully back together and you don't have the same privileges as before.

You see, what most guys do in this situation is take any validation from their ex as a sign that they're back together, causing them to rush into a relationship to end their anxiety and uncertainty of the future. They'll act jealous or use stalking behavior, which comes across as weakness and subtracts from their value. Their mentality is all about them and they care little about her experience, when and if she's ready. That kind of man will pressure her with the "What are we?" conversation too soon, before connection and intimacy are where it should be, all in an attempt to get her to fully commit and label the relationship too fervently. That is low-value thinking, which is downright unattractive and repels her.

These actions will only prove to her that she's still in control, that she is on a pedestal and has all of the power. He's just confirming that she made the right decision when she ended the relationship, causing her to shut herself off emotionally, think of him negatively, and cut any potential thought of a relationship with him in the future.

A high-value man, on the other hand, understands that his past relationship has ended. And even though a new relationship can form, it will take time, respecting both her space and his self-worth with unshakable patience.

Just as importantly, it requires mutual interest and effort. She needs to come back to you *on her own* in order for the relationship to have a long-term future. If you're the only one putting in effort and you feel like you're doing all the work and chasing her, then you are... and you must stop, pull back immediately and refocus on the core commitments.

High-pressure conversations and manipulation might work in the short term, causing her to come back out of pity or guilt because she does care about you, but eventually, she'll feel a proverbial buyer's remorse and you'll end up right back where you started or worse. So, how do you show her that you're a high-value man and that her life is better with you in it?

BE THE MAN AND STAY COMMITTED TO YOURSELF

No matter how many tools, tricks, or tactics you've heard from dating coaches and so-called gurus who promise to help you win your ex back with "three magical texts," the inescapable truth is this:

You cannot create a new relationship with your ex if you're showing up as the same man she broke up with.

The paradox here is that, to get her back for the long run, not just a month, you must first reach a place where you can look yourself in the eye and say, "I don't *need* her back."

You need to love yourself, your life, and the journeys you're on more than your ex. If your ex is your "everything," your reason for waking up, and the person who makes you feel whole and complete, you will repel her. Through your words, behaviors, and actions, you will reveal that you are *not* the prize to be won. She is. And if she's the prize, she has nothing to gain by coming back to you.

For the relationship to change, *you* must change. If you've been taking the core commitments seriously and fully internalizing and applying the lessons from this book, you're well on your way. But your journey doesn't stop simply because you're hooking up with your ex again. Although it might feel like it, it's just a milestone among many.

If your happiness is predicated on whether or not she comes back to you, mark my words, you will lose her. She wants to be with a man who is happy and thriving without her, who is on his *own* journey that she can happily join and benefit from. She doesn't want to be best part of your life which means she has little to gain.

More importantly, such a frame creates guaranteed suffering for *you* when you're not with her, leaving you wondering where she is, what she's doing and who she's doing it with. Her decision be damned, *you* must learn how to generate happiness and joy for your own sake. If you believe that "I cannot move forward and be happy unless this person is back in my life," you place conditions and constraints on your happiness and well-being that are *outside* of your control, which is a recipe for emotional suicide.

Instead of taking charge of your own emotional state and declaring to yourself, "I was happy before I met her, I can be happy without her," you give her complete power over your psychological, emotional, and spiritual state. You are at her mercy, and this is a burden that no one wants, let alone finds attractive.

Even if she does come back to you in this frame, you're still guaranteed to struggle. At the root, you're dependent on her for your joy and validation which will stifle your communication and behaviors. This dependency creates fear, weakness, and the slow death of your masculine spirit, the source of what attracts her to you. It leads to a relationship where you are "whipped," walking on eggshells, and seeing her as a goddess on a pedestal you must worship. With enough time, the fear of losing her love or approval will cause just as much suffering as the breakup did.

As challenging as it is, you must adopt the belief that "I can be happy on my own, and my ex (and other women) will ONLY be attracted to me when I'm happy, love myself, and am capable of thriving independent of any woman."

She's not the only option, she's one of many options. If you forget these truths because she's showing interest again, if you drop all of the habits and practices that allowed you to reclaim your power and attractiveness, the scales of power will quickly shift in her favor, causing a decrease in attraction.

So, as you begin to re-engage with your ex, continue focusing on the core commitments for yourself, not for her. Your life cannot be put on pause simply because she's showing interest. Keep advancing your career, developing skills, and working to build an amazing future for yourself. Show up to the gym and work to build your body and prioritize your health. Continue building a social network that is separate from her and occasionally say "no" to invitations from her so you can spend time with your own friends and family.

These are the actions that allowed you to re-attract her in the first place. And these are the actions that will allow you to *stay* attractive to her in your pursuit. She is not the prize, you are… so own it.

In addition to continuing the commitments and hard work you've put in up until this point, you need to stay on guard against the habits and behaviors that ended the relationship in the first place. Old habits die hard, and no matter how much work you've put in, your brain will try to push you back to homeostasis, your old and comfortable ways of being.

If the relationship ended because you took her for granted, became overly complacent, neglected her, were too needy or overly jealous, avoid these habits at all costs. If the relationship ended because of personal addictions or vices then, don't allow those vices to creep back in. If it ended because of dishonesty or infidelity, lead the relationship from an honest, trustworthy frame. Be as transparent as possible about anything that she *needs* to know if you're social with other women, dating or anything else she might care about.

THE TWO SCENARIOS THAT CAN DISMANTLE ALL PROGRESS

You must have a clear game plan for addressing triggering situations where it's possible you'll make weak irreversible choices. For most men, there are two primary scenarios that lead to unattractive behavior: their ex talking to unfamiliar men and intoxication.

First, with regards to your ex's involvement with other men, the solution is simple. *Act as if they don't exist or have any effect on you.* **You must have zero concern for the other men she's talking to.** Your frame is they are nothing more than annoying flies buzzing around her. You must know your value and understand the value of shared history and positive experiences, then you know pound for pound, *you* are the highest-value man in her life.

If you allow yourself to fall prey to jealous and needy behaviors, you're showing her that you aren't the prize, the *other* man is. The more attention you give other men in her life, the more she will gravitate away from you and toward them. Even if she might be intimate with another man, that doesn't mean it's over with you. Sometimes women need to experience what else is out there in order to understand your value and place in her life.

During my period of "no contact," I was intimate with other women, yet I still missed my ex. She may feel the same way if you remain calm and don't have emotional tantrums about the other men she's talking to.

Unless she is at the altar sharing wedding vows with an oversized belly, it's not over unless you decide it's over. Let these other men fall into the low-value, weak, needy, and chasing behaviors since she will likely be emotionally unavailable and they'll soon find out she's talking to other men including you, meanwhile you project strength, an abundance mentality and a respect of her boundaries and life choices.

Second, if alcohol or drugs use is a part of both your social lifestyles, I can tell you from personal experience that during the early stages of re-dating your ex, it's best to avoid or reduce these types of situations altogether. If you're on a date or at an event together, limit your alcohol consumption. If you're invited to a party or social gathering where you know alcohol and drugs will be involved, I encourage you to decline—increasing your perceived value and mystery—and make plans to do something else.

The risk vs. reward proposition is often weighed against you because, regardless of the substance you're using, the moment either one of you chemically alter your state, the chances of a negative interaction skyrocket. You may see her chatting with another guy, flirting, having fun, dancing, or taking pictures with other men, for example. And even though you may be able to keep your cool during a casual conversation where you're only talking about these scenarios, watching them play out in front of you with your own eyes (especially if you're intoxicated) is a completely different beast.

At the same time, she could also get drunk and unleash an emotional storm of repressed feelings that you don't know how to respond to. Or you may think things are going well, so after one drink too many, decide to bare your soul and tell her how much she means to you, how much you miss her, and how desperately you want her back.

Remember, attraction is like trust. It takes time to fully develop it, but it only takes seconds to ruin it. With a single emotional outburst, you can unravel all of the progress you've made with your ex and plunge your attraction to an all-time low, possibly losing her for good. For many men, this will lead to a snowball effect that unravels not only his progress with *her*, but the progress he's made in his life.

Unless she has specifically invited you to an event *as a couple* and you are going together, I encourage you to avoid these types of gatherings and situations for at least the first few months of re-dating (or at least until it's clear that you're "back together").

If you cannot go "together" and you feel the need to go to social events because your friends are also there (for example, a mutual friend's wedding), then do your best to minimize the role she plays in your evening. Have minimal contact and focus on having fun with your friends and not paying much attention to her. Let her come to you and be a part of your party and the fun you're creating, avoid hovering around her hoping anything good comes from being in her presence. Be the flame, not the moth.

THE HARDER YOU TRY, THE WORSE IT GETS

The more attached you are to the outcome of getting your ex back—an outcome that cannot be guaranteed or controlled—the harder you will try to force her back into your life. From this frame of desperation, you'll only push her further away. If you are chasing your ex, it implies that she is *running*. From this frame, you're in a place of scarcity, not abundance. You're saying, "I'm not good enough without you, I *need* you." And even if you "catch" her, you'll create a fragile foundation for your future relationship. You'll put in all of the work and effort but over time, you'll start to resent her for it. It isn't equal because you need her more than she needs you and you both know it.

The solution? Stop chasing. Let her be.

If you stop chasing, she will stop running. From this place, you can shift from scarcity into abundance and from pursuit into attracting her. This doesn't mean that you should simply sit at home playing video games and expect your ex to come back to you without *any* action.

Rather, you should take far less *direct* action than your anxious mind believes is necessary.

Remember, everything that you do should be filtered through the lens of value. What would a high-value man do? What would a low-value man do?

A low-value man has no options and few positive journeys or experiences that excite him. He would try to force his ex into a relationship the moment she shows interest. He'll put pressure on her, leading with the "What are we?" conversation and attempting to label the relationship before they've had the time and space to reattract and rediscover each other after the breakup. He'll use manipulation and high-pressure tactics—like bringing up all the times she said she loved him, wanted to marry him, or wanted to have a family—to try and force his way into her heart with past logic. None of this works.

The problem is that these conversations force her to relive the past (and all of the reasons that she fell out of love with you) *before* she has the opportunity to rebuild attraction in the present. Trying to define the relationship too soon only creates stress, anxiety, and pressure, and it detracts from all the value that you could bring into her life.

Regardless of her response, the low-value man dooms himself to failure because he's unable to show up as the attractive man she wants. If she responds positively, he'll overstay his welcome—staying too long at her place, bombarding her with texts and calls, giving her unnecessary gifts, and wearing his heart on his sleeve. If she responds negatively, he'll fight fire with more fire and resort to begging, pleading, and more chasing only making the situation worse.

But a high-value man understands that the most valuable action he can take is action on *himself*. This means working on the core commitments, improving his social life, health and fitness, career, and finances, and pursuing his passions. He understands that *she* is not the prize, *he* is. He knows that *she* must be the one chasing him, not him chasing her, stalking her, and showing up randomly like a crazy ex-boyfriend who has no self-control or care for her personal space and boundaries.

She cannot pursue you when you are chasing her.

If a woman is pursuing you, she is not going to get rid of you or stop thinking about you. Your attraction increases, even when you are not with her. She thinks about you at work, in traffic, and before bed.

Your life shouldn't drastically change after you begin seeing your ex again. You should not change your commitments, schedule, or important plans to make room for her... yet. Your goal is to take things slow and focus on *organically* rekindling connection, not forcing it with pressure and manipulation just to ease your own anxiety to rush back into a relationship.

You shouldn't work so hard to win her back, letting her consume your every thought, action, and behavior—even once you're dating her again—because even if she *never* comes back, your life is moving in an exciting direction and you can be happy without her.

Instead of rushing to label things and force a relationship, simply enjoy spending time together in each interaction. Be curious about who she's become since the breakup. Have fun as you learn about each other, share positive emotions together, and begin to grow those feelings for each other again.

Remember, your actions during these early interactions have more weight than your actions in the past. The way you are showing up now shows who you are today and what she can expect tomorrow.

During the first few weeks and even months that you're spending time together, avoid hanging out every day. A cadence of once a week or longer is a good start, then tighten it up. Be cautious not to overstay your welcome when together.

If you're overly eager, willing to do anything, or will cancel dinner with close friends or family to spend time with her, you're showing her that she is the prize. Be the one to leave before she asks, or politely tell her that you have plans later and she'll need to leave by a certain time. She's not in control of your schedule and you shouldn't drop your other obligations to stay with her longer. In fact, spending more but mediocre, connection-less time with her is not going to help you get her back. She needs to know that you have your own life going on in order for her to value the time she does get with you. She must re-earn being a priority in your life. At this point in your relationship, too much pointless time together can be deadly.

People value what they work hard for and what other people desire.

She will only value *you* if she invests her time, energy, and attention to have you in her life. She should feel uncertain about your feelings, as if she's not fully sure if she can win you over and needs to put in more effort to reattract you.

Allow your connection to build back slowly, giving her time to organically become attracted to you and giving you time to determine if she's the best long-term fit. The label of your relationship doesn't matter as much as how much value and attraction she feels for you today.

The "new you" knows that the goal is to feel like a couple before labeling and defining that you are a couple. When you finally define the relationship, it will be because it already exists and has existed for some time. You simply need to show up, have fun, and trust that with enough time, connection, and intimacy, a relationship will organically follow.

If you do this well, she'll be the one who initiates conversations about what you are as a couple and where you're going, just to ease her own anxiety about losing you. If *she's* the one leading these conversations, it shows that she's not only interested in you as a lover again, but she's ready to discuss the future. It's no longer a point of anxiety for her, but of curiosity. She's wanting *you* to clarify "What are we?" because she recognizes your newfound value as a man and wants to be a part of the life you're leading.

TAKE EXTREME OWNERSHIP OF THE PAST

Although the first few weeks you spend back together should be centered around fun, connection, adventure, and romance, once attraction is re-established and you're both more invested in each other as potential partners again, your shared history together will have to be addressed and acknowledged. The fun, adventure, and sex are an important precedent to resolving the past issues since her emotional attraction for you will have increased enough for her to care about solving them, but they aren't enough to heal the wounds you inflicted on each other in the past.

If you sweep your past under the rug and continue just going out to eat and having sex, you don't resolve anything. You allow the pains and traumas to fester like an infection. In the back of your minds, both of you will enter into every conversation feeling like "something" is off. If this goes on for too long, it will lead to disconnection, resentment, and likely the final closure of your relationship together.

Ideally, this conversation is initiated by *her*, not you. She needs to be ready to talk about the past and the potential for the future. Until her attraction for you has increased, you can't have a productive conversation about resolving the past or stepping into a new relationship together. However, depending on how the relationship ended and how deep the pain was for both of you, the responsibility may fall on your shoulders to lead the interaction.

When this conversation does happen, it's important for you to stay grounded, control your emotions, and genuinely validate and empathize with her experience. She needs to feel seen, heard, and respected. She needs to feel like there is a safe place where you can both communicate openly and resolve past problems *before* committing or attaching any labels. And it's likely that there will be many conversations about your previous relationship before she is willing to fully entertain the idea of getting back together.

As such, it's important that you establish a deep sense of safety from the onset of these conversations. Remember, it only takes one moment of weakness or one hurtful word to undo what you've built. So, no matter what she says or how it makes you feel, you *must* stay grounded, stay calm, and let her know that she can trust you.

At times, what she has to say may be too painful for you to bear in the moment. And that's okay. You're allowed to respectfully step away from the conversation by letting her know that you need to process and sit with what she's shared before responding. This doesn't mean you should storm out of the room screaming, "I can't talk about this right now!" but rather that you should calmly get up, hug her, and let her know:

"What you shared is a lot and my emotions are all over the place right now. I appreciate you trusting me enough to share what you just shared, and I want us to have a productive conversation about this. I just need a little time to collect myself and sit with everything so that I can respond with a clear head."

No matter how badly you want to resolve things and move forward, it's better to pause and step back and gather yourself than to rush forward when emotions are too heightened. With a single emotional outburst, you can shatter the container of safety, causing her to be worried about your response or fearful that you will lash out in anger. If so, she won't feel safe enough to confide in you. It's up to you to prove to her through your actions that she can trust you. She needs to know that she has the freedom to share her truth honestly, openly, and fully—and that you will do the same.

You don't want to argue, cast blame, or fight, which creates disconnection. You want to listen, empathize with, validate her emotions, and resolve issues, which creates connection. Remember, *both* of you got hurt. She was in love with you at one point, but somewhere along the way, that love began to fade.

She didn't get into the relationship expecting it to end. She never wanted the breakup to happen when she became your partner. Understanding that she was hurt just as badly as you were—even if the pain was experienced differently and at different times than you—will allow you to stay grounded even in the midst of heated emotional conversations.

During these conversations, it's important for you to be a leader and to own your mistakes. Don't hide behind excuses or cast blame on anyone other than yourself. If you made a mistake, then *own* it. More importantly, own how you're going to *fix* it (or even better, how you already have).

Always remember that these conversations will likely be the determining factor in whether or not your relationship works in the long term. If you can speak your truth with respect, understanding, and love and invite her to do the same, you will lay a new foundation for a new relationship that will be able to weather future storms.

Ultimately, what matters most is not the outcome of this process, but who you become as a result of going through it. Whether you get her back or decide together that you're both better off going your separate ways, you will emerge on the other side a stronger, more grounded, and more powerful man. An exciting future awaits.

BIG IDEAS:

1. **You must meet the requirements for reaching out.**
   I recommend waiting at least two to four months and discussing with several close friends and family members whether or not they believe you're in the right place mentally and emotionally to reconnect with her. Remember, you stand to lose more by rushing to reconnect than you do by waiting and focusing on yourself. If you reach out before you're strong and thriving, you will sabotage your chances of reconnecting with your ex.

2. **Let go of your expectations.**
   No matter who initiates contact, it's essential to remember that nothing has changed. You are not her partner, she is not yours. You are simply two former lovers who are reconnecting and learning about where each other is at post-breakup. Don't expect her to come rushing back to you or for the process of rekindling the romance to be smooth and easy. Both of you were hurt, and it will take time and patience to reestablish a connection.

3. **Take things slowly.**
   You must not *need* to get your ex back. Instead, you are simply exploring the option and trying to determine whether she's a possibility for you in the future. Don't rush to label things or pressure her with "What are we?" conversations. Instead, take things slowly, as if you're dating for the first time. Have fun, keep things casual, and be the first to leave. Trust that a few positive interactions will be worth far more than dozens of mediocre touch points.

4. **Pay attention to your ex's actions to determine whether a relationship is possible.**
   Look at how she's grown (or hasn't) and how she's spent her time as a newly single woman. Her actions will be the greatest indicator of whether or not there's the potential for a future relationship, not her words.

5. **Decide from a place of values and abundance, not scarcity and fear.**
   After the first few interactions and conversations, you will likely reach a point where you know whether or not your ex is the right fit for you long term. But it's easy to allow the emotional pull and attachment to cloud your judgment, especially if sex is involved so soon. Step back and give yourself time and space away from her to think through the recent interactions and the idea of a possible relationship with an objective lens. Is she a good fit for your life based on your values and vision for the future?

   If so, then move forward and reinvent your relationship together. If not, accept reality with grace, take the lessons, and trust that with enough focus on the core commitments, you'll find the great partner when ready.

A FEW LAST WORDS

You have a choice between allowing this experience to define you—to be broken, defeated, turning to vices and distractions to escape from the hurt—and rising *above* the pain and finding meaning in it, learning from it, and using it as fuel to propel you into a greater life.

Even though it's a harder path to pursue, it's the path where you'll find your freedom. And through this journey, you're reborn as a strong grounded man, a man who is more alive and joyful *because* of this experience, not in spite of it. You have a choice to rise, to grow, and to build a beautiful life, one day at a time.

You must choose to live.

WANT TO HELP MEN GOING THROUGH A BREAKUP?

I am on a mission to impact the lives of 1,000,000 men going through one of the most painful experiences of their life with this book – but I can't do it alone.

So, if you've found this book helpful on your journey, please pay it forward by taking one minute to write a helpful review on Amazon to ensure this book makes it into the hands of as many men who need it.

Together we can end the pain, suffering, and loneliness with which so many men going through breakups experience, one man at a time.

Stay Grounded,

Andrew Ferebee
Founder of Knowledge For Men

Check out my cult classic book: "The Dating Playbook For Men" on Amazon

Want my help? Learn more about the incredible work I do with men at: knowledgeformen.com/grow

Printed in Great Britain
by Amazon

44549613R00101